THE PHANTOM BRIGADE

THE PHANTOM BRIGADE

or

The Contemptible Adventurers

A. P. G. VIVIAN

The Naval & Military Press Ltd

Published by

The Naval & Military Press Ltd

Unit 5 Riverside, Brambleside
Bellbrook Industrial Estate
Uckfield, East Sussex
TN22 1QQ England

Tel: +44 (0)1825 749494

www.naval-military-press.com
www.nmarchive.com

FOREWORD

In writing the story of *The Phantom Brigade*, I have endeavoured to portray the experiences of most of the men who silently left England on the outbreak of the Great War, with the original British Expeditionary Force, and to present a unique phase of the war, the conditions of which were never again met with during the whole of the remainder of the time it was in progress.

It is based entirely on actual experience, and covers a period from the 4th August, 1914, to 3rd September, 1914.

The conduct of the war in those early days, of which very little, or nothing, has been written, will probably supply a new and interesting outlook on that greatest of all contests, to everybody, except the comparative few of the first one hundred thousand who emerged from the War unscathed.

A. P. G. V.

CONTENTS

THE PHANTOM BRIGADE

CHAPTER I

August the Fourth, Nineteen Fourteen.

A RED letter day in the lives of us all, and, at the time, especially regarded as such by the Regular serving soldier of the period, for it signified the realisation of his most cherished ambition—Engagement on Active Service.

To revert a few years, I, at the tender age of fourteen, prompted by the possession of a lively spirit of adventure, left my kind parents and a jolly comfortable home, and enlisted in the Army, in May, 1907.

Within a couple of hours of my attestation, I was on my way, *en route* to join my regiment in Londonderry, Ireland.

I started off on that journey from London, clad in a uniform a large number of sizes too big for me, feeling the proudest boy in the Empire.

My pride suffered a severe setback when, during a break in the journey, I was discovered by a huge and kindly policeman, sobbing out my heart in a decidedly unsoldierlike manner, in a back street in Belfast.

I had contrived to become hopelessly lost when attempting to pass away the time, whilst waiting for a connecting train to my destination, by exploring that city.

Visions of courts-martial and the sentences of death by shooting, presumably awarded by them to all deserters, had chased themselves across my childish imagination, and reduced me to the final stages of horror, these visions, doubtless, being the outcome of a certain brand of literature popular among schoolboys of my day.

The kindly assurance of the policeman that I had been lost but a few minutes, and that I had ample time to catch my train, calmed my fear and restored me to a more manly mien, and it was a somewhat proud and happy boy that subsequently made known his arrival in the Army.

On that memorable 4th August, I was serving at Devonport in the ranks of the 4th Battalion the Middlesex Regiment, which was one of the units composing the 8th Infantry Brigade, 3rd Division.

We had, of course, read of the trouble brewing on the Continent, which, to us, was a far-distant and unexplored region, and had regarded it with a mild interest not unmixed with envy of the lucky troops of the nations involved, for never, for a moment, did it enter our heads that we would be affected in any way.

As the hot August days wore on, rumours, daily ever growing stronger, of the possibility of Britain taking up the cudgels, became so rife and convincing that, by the Fourth, our erstwhile mild interest had changed into sensations of the liveliest excitement.

When I revert, through the years that have elapsed, to that day, I see every event with a crystal-like clearness.

I distinctly remember that it was a broiling day, and the band of the regiment, of which I was a member

and a Corporal of the Lance to boot, was engaged in
practice.

The bandmaster was essaying the hopeless task of
chaining our thoughts, which were exclusively engaged in the realms of the romance and glamour of
the great adventure looming largely before us, to the
exercise of a musical programme which he intended
us to inflict upon a long-suffering public later on in
the day.

Our agony was suddenly relieved by the appearance
of a very excited orderly-sergeant who, after unceremoniously thrusting open the door of the practice
room shrieked out an order that we were to repair to
our respective companies, to prepare for mobilisation,
without delay.

Utterly demoralised by this command, which was
greeted with uncontrolled whoops of mad joy, we
abandoned all thoughts of discipline, threw down our
instruments, and turned in a body to dash from the
room.

The cold voice of authority outraged, issuing from our
immediate superior officer, the bandmaster, arrested
our headlong flight, and, obeying his stern order, considerably crestfallen, we resumed our former places.

In a voice thrilling with sarcasm and indignation at
our action, which we had wrongly assumed without
reference to his instructions in the matter, he coldly
gave us his opinion, and asked:

'Why are you so eager to prepare yourselves to be
slaughtered? Are you tired of life, or is your undis-
ciplinary conduct due to sheer ignorance? You are

anxious to go to war, but believe me, my lads, there is nothing nice about war, I guarantee you that the moment you have had your first taste of it you will be a damned sight more anxious to get back here.'

These wise words were received by us, in our sublime ignorance, with great scorn, for we were not, at that time, in a position to appreciate their sterling merit.

War—in spite of all the dreadful things written and spoken about it—will always exercise its glamour and fascination over the uninitiated, which nothing but actual participation in conflict will destroy.

You cannot successfully warn the inexperienced person against war any more than you can persuade an infatuated bachelor to avoid the pitfalls of matrimony.

In either case you will find that he will treat your earnest advice with contempt. Firmly convinced that you, with your good intentions and desire for his welfare, are a consummate liar, he becomes the more eager to rush to his undoing.

The prospects of a war, or of a wife, apparently affect a man in the same manner; they blind him to common sense and realities.

After all, perhaps this phenomenon can be readily understood when we consider that experience of both show a distinct similarity, in that each invariably lead to a shattering of ideals, and a life of strife.

The arrival of another harassed non-commissioned officer, with the repetition of an order to us to report for mobilisation without further delay, could no longer be ignored by the bandmaster, and on receipt of his permission, very grudgingly given, we left the band-room in a wild charge towards our respective company headquarters.

I arrived breathlessly, filled with an apprehensive idea that the regiment was on the verge of moving off to wage the war without me, which, to my unbounded relief, I found erroneous.

The Company Quartermaster-Sergeant took me in hand and conducted me into a spare barrack room, that had been converted into a mobilisation store, filled to overflowing with arms and accoutrements. Here I was speedily issued with the additional kit and equipment that a soldier receives only upon mobilisation for Active Service.

The acquisition of these articles thrilled me with pleasurable sensations, and, upon arriving back in my barrack-room, I spread them out and contemplated them at great length with feelings of awe, paying particular tribute of that nature to the packet containing the field dressings, designed to cover any gory wounds a soldier might receive in the course of action.

Thus prepared, I was exceedingly anxious to start away to the war without further loss of time.

I, at this phase, suffered a great disappointment which many may fail to appreciate.

I was appointed to the command of a stretcher-bearing party, which meant that, to all intents and purposes, I was to take part in the forthcoming struggle as a non-combatant.

This appointment was a great blow to me, especially as I was, at that time, the best rifle shot in my

B

company, and very keen on exercising my prowess in that capacity.

Unfortunately, at least as I considered, some little time before the outbreak of hostilities I had passed, with honours, through a course of instruction in the art of rendering first aid, consequently, all my endeavours to escape the new duty thrust, unsought, upon me, failed.

Immediately after the declaration of war, the reservists, necessary to build the battalion up to its full war strength, began to stagger along.

I use the word stagger in its literal sense, as that describes the manner in which the majority of them arrived, for it was obvious that on their journey to the regiment, they had been the recipients of much attention from the public—'Public' in more than one sense.

We observed the arrival of these reinforcements, during the daylight hours, with appreciation and a great deal of amusement.

Our point of view changed, however, to feelings of rage and annoyance concerning them, when, after night had enveloped us, we were repeatedly startled from our sleep by the awful noises with which the air resounded, as these tardy arrivals at the barracks strove to render their repertoire of maudlin songs of love and defiance.

The mornings would present us with an amazing sight. Hundreds of these happy adventurers would be seen littering the barrack-square, in all manner of grotesque attitudes, slumbering blissfully and peacefully where they had dropped in their tracks during the preceding night.

At the sound of the first note of 'Reveille' a swarm of non-commissioned officers would rush forth and pounce upon these warriors who lay smiling sweetly in their calm repose, sweetly that is, until they were rudely restored to things material and a bitter realisation that all the pleasures of this life must be paid for, by a none too gentle shaking.

It was at this time that I witnessed a spectacle but rarely observed in a well-disciplined corps.

The sergeant in command of the main guard had, evidently, allowed himself during the night, to be overcome by the 'spirits' of some of these Reservists; consequently, when the orderly officer of the day 'turned out' the guard in the morning he was presented with the astonishing sight of the sergeant of the guard standing solemnly at the salute on the right of his guard, holding a dripping and filthy mop in lieu of his rifle.

The spirit of abandonment entered most of us during those hectic days, but, fortunately, although not considered by us in that light at the time, our will to run amok was curtailed by a painful shortage of cash.

The emoluments of the soldier of pre-war days left him a long, long way behind the millionaire class.

I remember, with ungodly pleasure, that I did manage to wangle one glorious fling before the regiment departed for the Front.

It happened, unexpectedly, in this way:

A couple of nights before we left England I sat in a barrack-room with my chum, a bright young lad named Palmer, nicknamed 'Pedler,' as is the case with all army 'Palmers,' in earnest conference.

We were attempting to arrive at a decision as to the best and most advantageous manner in which we could squander a sum of eighteen pence that we had managed to raise after many anxious and diplomatic moments spent with the plutocrats of the battalion.

The advent of a party of men who proceeded to open up and engage in the time-honoured game of 'Pontoon' brought an end to our dilemma, and we joined in the game with our small stake, with surprisingly satisfactory results.

After an hour's play, our eighteen pence had grown into a sum well exceeding two pounds, which, to us, was the wealth of Midas.

We had thus, to our unbounded astonishment 'broken the bank,' or, in other words, the poor devils who had been opposed to our luck, and we discreetly retired with our ill-gotten gains, and fared forth into the town to enjoy one of the most glorious nights of our existence.

The end of this most perfect day synchronised with the appearance of a large squad of military policemen, who, displaying a distinct lack of humour, tore us from the ranks of a Salvation Army Band, with whom we were performing as the star attractions, and guided us, sorely against our wills, to our little grey home in the West Country.

On or about the eighth day of August the last Reservist had reported for duty, and the battalion was at last at its full fighting strength of, approximately, one thousand officers and other ranks.

The mobilisation of the battalion was thus completed and we were ready to take the 'field' at a moment's notice.

Now passed a time of anxious waiting for the arrival of our orders to depart, which was filled in by military exercises, particularly those of a marching nature.

We were introduced to this 'donkey' work side of Active Service by progressive stages.

The first day of these trials we took a little stroll of about fifteen miles, loaded with every stitch of our equipment and each one of the miscellaneous articles of ironmongery with which a soldier is cursed.

On each subsequent day the length of the march was increased a few more miles, until even the most pacific of us yearned for the comparative relief of more pleasant action we hoped to experience in a good, bloodthirsty 'scrap.'

Returning to our barracks after these jaunts, looking and feeling considerably less martial than on our setting forth earlier in the day, we would anxiously seek the latest news on the progress of the war, suffering all the time an awful apprehension that we would discover that the hot-headed French had selfishly concluded it on their own during the few hours we had been away upon our ramble.

With our minds relieved on this point we would gather in groups and heatedly discuss the military situation, wherein each debater with an air of a successful Commander-in-Chief, would unfold, to his own unbounded satisfaction, the strategy he would employ to bring the conflict to an abrupt and highly satisfactory conclusion.

The day or two preceding our departure from Plymouth, we were all confined to our barracks, which made the days seem long, and the evenings longer.

The latter we whiled away in the regimental canteen, singing, and, in some few cases, drinking.

It may cause surprise to learn that in those brave days the majority of us were staunch teetotallers; this state of affairs being produced by the fact that drink, other than water, could not be obtained without payment in cash.

As I reflect upon this period I can picture the awful expressions of anguish depicted on the countenances of the men who, unfortunately, lacked the means that would enable them to obtain the nourishment they deemed the most essential to their well-being, as they sat, gazing appealingly, and with intense longing, at their more fortunate comrades.

As these days of waiting dragged slowly along, revealing no signs of real action to our painfully anxious minds, we became depressed, and began to entertain thoughts that our Allies did not consider our services necessary to aid them in the war.

The reports of the wonderful victories gained by the Belgians at Liège caused us especial concern. Not that we, for a single moment, begrudged them their successes, but they filled us with a fear that our fond and misguided hopes of experiencing the 'chivalrous romance' of the war would be dashed to the ground.

We retired to our beds each night, hoping and praying that the morrow would bring us our marching and sailing orders.

At long last they came on the night of the twelfth of August, and were received by all with acclamations and expressions of the maddest excitement. We were destined to leave for the scene of operations on the morning of the thirteenth.

Not a wink of sleep for any of us on that marvellous night.

In the early morning, just before we paraded upon our barrack square for the last time, I stood in the company of our chaplain.

As he gazed upon the excited troops, he said:

'I thank God for His mercy in hiding the future from them and thus enabling them to face their forthcoming ordeal with so much cheerfulness. They, happily, do not realise what war means and that very few of them will ever see the skies of England again.'

This little homily had a distinctly depressing and disquieting effect upon me, and I made haste to leave him and join more congenial company.

Subsequent events proved that he was possessed of remarkable powers of prophecy.

Eventually the great moment arrived, and we paraded, and then started upon the first stage of our journey to the scene of the Great Adventure.

Preceded by the band of the Royal Marines of Plymouth, we proudly swung through the admiring crowds to the railway station.

This was the most heroic moment of my young life.

Arriving at the station, we speedily entrained, and amid the tumultuous cheers of the throngs of citizens and citizenesses of the 'Three Towns',who had gathered to wish us 'God speed', our train bore us away.

All our movements were wrapped in the deepest veil of secrecy, therefore we did not have the faintest idea which port of embarkation we were making for, and a long and tedious journey ensued.

Packed like the proverbial sardine in carriages rendered unbearable by the heat of a scorching sun, we travelled for hours toward our unknown destination, with scarcely a stop, until we eventually found ourselves beside a harbour crowded with all manner of ships.

Here we received, with feelings of great relief and delight, an order to detrain, and discovered that we had arrived at Southampton.

In a very short space of time, with very little fuss, we embarked upon one of the smallest ships that has ever been launched.

At least, that was the impression I gathered, judging from the difficulty we experienced in getting ourselves all neatly stowed aboard.

The majority of us managed to find seating accommodation only after a great deal of manœuvring, and by packing ourselves one behind the other, after the style adopted by pillion riders.

Having squeezed myself into position, I discovered that our activities were so limited that I could not get at my water-bottle that was hanging in its allotted place at my side.

On this occasion, as on most others, it contained for my refreshment the very best beer procurable, so the hardship inflicted upon me by this crowded state of affairs will be, no doubt, readily appreciated.

As soon as the last man had been deftly inserted aboard our little ship, we set sail, and quietly stole down through Southampton Water as the landmarks were becoming obscured by the darkness of the night.

Although the weather was comparatively calm, some of those hardy soldier men began to interest themselves in 'The Call of the Sea.'

At this point, the disadvantages of our compressed state became painfully apparent.

The expressions on the faces of the unfortunate men who found themselves the recipients of the tribute poured out by those who had found it impossible to resist the aforesaid 'Call of the Sea' would have given an onlooker great entertainment, provided, unlike we poor folk, he had no reason to fear that every moment might see him plunged into a similar predicament.

Of a necessity, immovable, they sat, perfect models of strong, silent men, only able to register their disgust and anger through their eyes, which bulged with a hopeless despair.

It was not recognised, or appreciated in the right spirit at the time, but those silent heroes were undergoing an experience which prepared them for the ordeal they were to face within a few days, and which enabled them to withstand the fury of the enemy's bombardments with so much fortitude.

All through the sultry night of the twelfth-thirteenth of August, we sailed hither and thither, attended jealously by a lean destroyer, which constantly swept around us in circles, thus providing us with the comforting assurance our senior sister service was very much 'on the job.'

As the dawn dispersed the veil of night, we saw that we were standing in towards land, and the few of us who found it possible, surveyed the coastline eagerly.

Where in the wide world were we?

Surely we could not have arrived off the shores of France so soon!

CHAPTER II

F<small>RANCE</small>, indeed it was, we were informed, and our eyes were riveted to its sunny shores as we slowly approached, until, through the slight mist, we were able to discern the shadowy arms of a pier, or breakwater, which we learned protected the entrance of the port of Boulogne, our destination.

Immediately the air became filled with our exclamations of wonder and interest, childish in their simplicity, at this first glimpse of the country that bore a name that had been familiar to us from the earliest days of our childhood. The country that had given birth to some of the most romantic figures of history.

Our own regimental colour bore witness to many a bloody strife between our predecessors and the valiant sons of France; indeed, it was in a particularly sanguinary contest with them that the regiment earned the nickname, of which we were immoderately proud, —'The Diehards.'

In this manner I mused as, agog with excitement at the thought of the Great Adventure looming before us, we drew in to the coast.

The rising sun, penetrating the slight mist here and there, gilded some of the windows of the buildings of the port we were nearing, causing them to reflect jolly twinkling lights, spelling to us goodwill and welcome.

Our straining eyes suddenly noted the appearance of two slim, graceful craft, which swept into our view from behind the protecting arm of the breakwater.

They dashed towards us, and then circled gaily around and around us, while their crews, occupying every position of vantage, cheered us wildly.

They were two torpedo-boat-destroyers of the navy of France.

We responded to their cheers with great heartiness, and tried to convey to them the spirit that animated us, for we, with a colossal conceit, imagined that with our arrival the war was as good as won, and that the worry and trials of our Allies were over.

One of the destroyers, apparently impressed by our obvious optimism, swerved towards the mouth of the harbour, and disappeared from our sight, no doubt to spread the good tidings to their fellow countrymen ashore.

We sailed past the long arm of the pier which was occupied by an immense throng, composed of the citizens of Boulogne, who accorded us a stirring welcome, recording their pleasure at our advent in no uncertain terms, by indulging in frenzied shouts, and the wildest gesticulations imaginable.

Our particular attention was claimed by a huge jovial-looking old gentleman, who bore a peculiar-shaped moustache which imparted to his features an unmistakable resemblance to a walrus.

He shouted and pranced about in such a manner that we were compelled to shriek with laughter, and he was unanimously voted to be the 'star' turn of the show.

This judgment was justified when he, evidently aware of his likeness to the above-mentioned sea-beast, apparently decided to live up to it, and dived, a clawing, shrieking heap, into the sea beneath.

As he was quickly salvaged, apparently none the worse for his untimely immersion, with his fervour undiminished, we showed our unqualified approval of the humorous diversion he had staged for our benefit, by a rousing cheer, which he acknowledged with graceful bows and smirks.

We eventually drew alongside a berth that had been specially prepared for us, and made fast amid the shrieking of the sirens of the shipping assembled in the port.

Eagerly filled with consuming curiosity, we struggled for vantage points that would enable us to obtain an uninterrupted view of the quay side.

The shore alongside the ship was packed by a teeming, clamouring crowd of all ages and sexes.

The strange words that floated up to us and smote our unaccustomed ears we found irresistibly funny, and we greeted them with uncouth laughter.

We observed, drawn up in front of the crowd, a body of men, and from their appearance, we, at first, assumed that they were the male chorus from a local production of 'The Chocolate Soldier.'

Their martial appearance, however, and their possession of exceedingly businesslike-looking rifles and bayonets dispersed that idea, and we at last recognised that they were real soldiers.

They were a guard of honour, part of a French infantry battalion, and our original impression

perhaps may be excused by the fact that they were
the first continental soldiers we had ever seen, and,
their gaudy uniforms appeared distinctly unusual to
the eye of the British soldier.

They were clothed in baggy pantaloons of a startling
red hue, sky blue greatcoats, having the bottoms of
the front fastened back, giving them a swallow-tailed
effect, and funny little hats topped with red.

Naturally, as soon as we realised that these men were
members of the army of our Allies, we gave them our
undivided attention.

I was considerably surprised to note that they all
appeared to be a great deal older than we were. Most
of them concealing their features behind tremendous
growths of a hirsute nature, which gave to them a
particularly ferocious aspect.

With this discovery, I glanced around at the boyish
faces of my comrades, all conspicuously innocent of
hair, and my review caused me to entertain a fear
that our French friends would imagine that we were
a contingent of Boy Scouts, and would be, accordingly, as much amused at our appearance as we had
been at theirs, but with more justification.

My fears upon this point were set at rest when, on
closer acquaintance, I found that they were old veterans
who had rejoined the Colours immediately upon the
first threat of war, for service with third-line units, thus,
by this action, securing the release of the younger and
more active men for service in the front line.

This knowledge caused us to regard them with unbounded admiration and respect.

All preparations having at last been completed, we received orders to disembark, and on landing endeavoured to arrange ourselves in parade order.

This operation proved extraordinarily difficult, owing to the friendly attentions of the vast throng assembled to greet us.

Some of us, indeed, were kidnapped and drawn into the surging crowd, and were only rescued by the zeal displayed by scores of ferocious-looking gendarmes, who almost quartered us as they tore us from our admirers, and restored us to our proper sphere.

At last, after almost superhuman efforts on the part of our officers, ably seconded by our good friends, the gendarmes, we were formed into some kind of order, and the battalion was ready to move.

I must explain here that, at this point of my story, I held a little command, which consisted of eight stretcher bearers, carrying between them four stretchers.

Immediately before the battalion started, I was ordered to have the stretchers packed on the company wagon, and to remain behind with my men who were required to unload munitions from the s.s. *Mombasa*, the ship in which we had crossed from England to France.

At first we considered this news very tough luck, and a number of my men exercised the soldier's well-known prerogative, but happily it proved a simple and most delightful task, for, on comprehending the nature of the duties allotted us, our good colleagues of the French guard of honour begged us to allow them the privilege and pleasure of deputising for us.

By no means loth to grant such gallant and considerate men the boon they so earnestly craved, we acceded to their request, to our mutual satisfaction.

While they were thus amusing themselves, we, having nothing better to occupy our time, stood around, feeling very heroic, accepting the adoration of the people there assembled.

As in duty bound, we did our utmost to place the *entente* upon a firm and satisfactory basis, an occupation that proved thoroughly enjoyable, as the greater number of the crowd were members of the fair sex.

In a miraculously short space of time I was given to understand that the munitions had been safely transferred from the ship to the vehicle destined to bear them away.

Having thus been deprived of any further excuse for remaining in our delightful surroundings, we enthusiastically shook all our new soldier friends by the hand, and after endeavouring to convey our thanks to them for their good work we reluctantly attempted to follow in the wake of the battalion.

I say attempted advisedly, for it quickly became apparent that progress of any sort was utterly impracticable.

We discovered that we formed the core of a struggling, enthusiastic mass of humanity.

I judged, by the pressure to which we were being subjected, that we were in the midst of most of the inhabitants of France.

These good people were determined to show us how much they appreciated us, although in their attempts to display their affection they almost succeeded in crushing the life out of us.

Eventually, by a stroke of good fortune, the tide turned, and set us all drifting in the general direction it was our duty to go.

I had received instructions to rejoin the battalion on the completion of the task at the quay, at St. Martin's Camp, and, having ascertained the route, we proceeded on our way at the rate of about one yard per hour.

We were progressing, inch by inch, when suddenly, to our infinite relief, one side of the accompanying crowd collapsed.

Upon moving into the cavity thus formed, we were agreeably surprised to discover ourselves in a shop-like structure, in which refreshments were being dispensed. This, we learned, was known as a café.

We soon discovered that it had become impossible to leave owing to the fact that the exit was completely blocked by the crowd of well-intentioned citizens, who were all striving to get inside for the purpose of pledging us their good will.

We certainly boosted the *Entente Cordiale* that day, especially the cordial part.

The time passed pleasantly in this manner, and eventually the little matter of rejoining our regiment assumed such trivial proportions that it was deemed unworthy of our consideration and attention.

Someone started a mechanical organ, whereupon we, initiating the ladies into London customs, changed headgear with them, and indulged in wild dances,

c

and, in fact, behaved ourselves to the prejudice of good order and military discipline generally.

Alas! all good things have a nasty habit of terminating unpleasantly.

The jollification had reached its zenith when an interruption occurred in the form of a posse of our dear old military police.

They had, no doubt, been attracted by the crowd, and upon hearing ejaculations that had certainly never originated from the French, had investigated, and had discovered our presence in the midst of that merry party.

Prompted by the cursed spirit of prohibition, they commanded us to cease our revels, and to take leave of our friends.

We ignored their exhortations, whereupon they made a determined attack upon our position, and after a terrific, and more or less bloody, struggle, they succeeded in tearing us from the bosoms of our delightful French pals.

Under their kindly guidance, we arrived at our destination, the camp, in which we found our battalion.

Here the police consigned us to the tender mercies of the sergeant of the guard, who greeted us with a glare of undisguised envy.

Having, apparently, been thrown off his normal balance by the sight of us, he omitted to take disciplinary action, but contented himself with gasping out an order to us 'to get to hell out of his sight.'

This order we promptly obeyed with thankful hearts, for we still possessed enough sense to realise that we had been exceedingly fortunate in escaping the more serious consequences of our undisciplined conduct.

I tacked away, feeling very happy, thinking how delightful were the conditions of Active Service. From a regular soldier's point of view, far better than those of peace.

I arrived at the entrance of a tent, and as the interior looked inviting, I entered, and dropped comfortably to the floor, where I slid gratefully into the healing arms of Morpheus.

My pleasant slumbers were rudely disturbed by the harsh sounds of an unbearable voice, and a series of vicious thumps about my anatomy.

Gradually I awoke to the realisation that the irate, and never-to-be-forgotten face of the Company Quartermaster-Sergeant was hovering over me, emitting a strong line in swear words.

I gathered from his remarks, after they had been sifted and all the unnecessary adjectives had been discarded, that I had selected as my couch his ration of bread and, so-called, butter, which he had an urge for.

I tried to explain that I had endeavoured to do my best in view of his 'pressing' need, but my excuses availed me nothing, and I was unfeelingly ejected from that tent.

Once outside, I made the discovery that, for some unaccountable reason, I was feeling distinctly unwell, so I decided to take a stroll through the camp in the hope that fresh air would effect an improvement in my condition.

My attention was attracted by a huge column, surmounted by a statue, not unlike our monument to Nelson in Trafalgar Square.

This assumed signal interest to me when I was informed by a lady standing near me, who, to my surprise spoke English fluently, that it was a memorial erected to the memory of the immortal Napoleon.

There he stood, in effigy, awesome in his majestic loneliness, gazing out across the Channel towards the white cliffs of England, the country he had vainly striven to conquer.

My interest, already deeply roused, was considerably increased when my fair informant kindly explained that at this spot, near to the camp now occupied by the British troops, Napoleon had assembled the great army with which he intended to invade our shores.

I stood in deep reverie, musing upon this information.

When, in my schooldays, grappling with history, I had read of this mighty army and its avowed purpose, never for an instant did I imagine that I would, one day, stand upon the site of their encampment as a British soldier, no longer an enemy, but as a friend and ally of their descendants, pledged to aid them in the defence of their beloved country, against a common foe.

A series of clarion calls interrupted my thoughts, and I turned away, and went back to our camp to ascertain the cause of the tumult.

I found that everybody was rushing about in a state of high excitement, and learnt that the battalion had received orders to prepare to leave for an unknown destination, somewhere in France.

After some little trouble I managed to collect my weighty equipment, being mildly surprised to find it intact, and repaired to parade my party.

Upon calling the roll of my little command, I was pained to discover that there was an absentee.

I awaited his appearance for some time, until signs that the battalion was about to march were imminent, and still he tarried.

I instituted a search for him.

Almost immediately, sounds of ribald mirth emanating from some of the members of the search party drew me in their direction, where I found displayed the cause of their laughter.

The missing man lay reclining blissfully upon the bank of a ditch, which obviously functioned as the main drain for the camp, with his lower extremities immersed in the evil flood.

He slept, fully accoutred, wearing a happy smile of utmost content.

Heaven alone knows the motive that had induced him to select this peculiar resting place, but I assumed that his unfortunate choice had been due to 'blind' ignorance.

I could not imagine how he was able to remain so oblivious to his unpleasant surroundings, and, pityingly, I endeavoured to restore him to awful consciousness by the judicious application of the toe of my boot.

That my ministrations had the desired effect I was soon informed by the expression of loathing that succeeded his erstwhile happy mien.

I sadly instructed him to join us as soon as possible, and the remainder of us hurriedly departed for our parade post.

The battalion left the camp, and we moved slowly down into, and through the town, our party forming the rearguard, as it were.

In this position we were exposed to great temptations, as again members of the crowd tried to cut us off and bear us away with them to indulge in light refreshment.

We sternly resisted these well-meant attentions, however, as we realised that another escapade similar to that we had enjoyed earlier, would, without doubt, be visited with severe punishment.

A still stronger motive kept us to the strait and narrow path, for, as far as we knew, we were about to leave for the scene of action, and not one of us would have forgone his chance of participating in a battle for anything on earth.

Not at that time.

Our immediate destination proved to be the railway station.

Here we speedily stowed ourselves away in a train composed of real passenger carriages, not the 40 Hommes-8 Chevaux boxes that were the lot of troops in later days.

This revelation will prove to soldiers of the Great War how popular we were with the powers that were of the Boulogne of those far-off days.

A considerable wait ensued upon our occupation of the train. Those of my party found this exceedingly

irksome, a feeling, I understand, that was not experienced by other members of the battalion, for it would
appear that some of the bolder damsels of Boulogne
entered some of the compartments of the train, and
proceeded to entertain their occupants.

Judging from the unmistakable sounds that occasionally emanated from these compartments, I
gathered that the inmates were indulging in 'petting
parties'.

It was at this point that we discovered that we had
'shipped' a 'Jonah.'

Our sleepy friend of the ditch episode became rather
objectionable, and we commanded him to sit as near
to the door and the open air as possible, deeming that
in such a position he would be the least offensive.

Unfortunately our strategy proved to be at fault.

A few bright-eyed girls were observed tripping ex-
pectantly towards us.

Arriving at the threshold of our carriage, they
beamed sweetly and invitingly upon us.

With shocking abruptness their saucy smiles turned
into looks of puzzled, painful surprise, and, clutching
desperately at their pretty noses, they, to our intense
chagrin, sped away into the night.

At first their conduct was inexplicable, until we
realised that we had with us in that compartment,
something far more potent than 'The Gipsy's
Warning.'

Angrily we glared at the cause of our discomfiture.

'Pedler,' gulping down his tears of disappointment,
sobbed for my permission to strangle the 'Jonah,'

which was heartily accorded, but he was unable to carry out his laudable purpose, the offender proving too strong for him in more than one sense.

At long last, with the railway officials producing prodigies of noise from the comic little trumpets beloved of them, the train, with an excellent imitation of a cocktail-shaker, started off.

We travelled all through that 'scented' night full of speculation as to our goal and the chances of our being involved in an engagement in the early morning.

Such was our general knowledge of the military situation.

CHAPTER III

The darkness of night, hiding the view and characteristics of the country through which we were passing was at last broken by the first grey streaks of dawn.

Dormant interests in our surroundings at once revived and we all began to sit up and take notice once more.

All the platforms of the stations through which we flew were crowded by persons, mostly women and children, who did us the honours right well.

They waved and shrieked at us, the main theme of their shrieks being a shrill 'Heep! Heep! Heep!' finishing abruptly on the last 'Heep!' This caused me an uncomfortable sensation of tenseness that is indescribable. It left something wanting. That it had a similar effect on the others, I understood, when one of them leaned out of the window and yelled:

'For Jake's sake shout "Hurrah"!'

It never came, however, and we decided that the omission was due to a flaw in their methods of education.

We now began to feel the promptings of the inner man, and turned to some preserved rations with which we had been issued before leaving Boulogne.

The ration was supposed to be allotted at the ratio of one very small tin per two hungry, hulking soldiers.

Unfortunately, as quartermaster-sergeants have never been known to err on the generous side, we only received four tins to be shared between nine of us. The odd man of our party causing us to be worse off than we might have been, besides providing us with a problem when it came to making divisions. As far as I have been able to discover, this sort of niggardly conduct on the part of quartermaster-sergeants is their only means of justifying their existence.

We arrived at a solution of our mathematical dilemma by tossing by pairs, for the odd man.

What a series of jolts and surprises those little tins had in store for us.

'Pedler' and I eagerly opened ours.

'Holy Moses!' shrieked 'Pedler', when the contents were revealed, 'We're unlucky, we've clicked something gone bad.'

It certainly appeared a bit of a mess, but on closer examination it turned out to be a really excellent apple dumpling.

A shout of glee heralded the discovery of the contents of another tin.

This showed ready-cooked rashers of bacon and eggs. The joy of the owners of this can was somewhat damped by the memory of the fact that it had to be shared three ways, they having won the odd man of the party.

The other two revealed herrings in tomato sauce, and another apple dumpling respectively.

We were rather surprised to find the food in such excellent condition, it being a popular supposition among us that they were surplus stores of the Crimean or other old war.

After a conference, it was decided to pool the whole lot, and we enjoyed a fruity breakfast, consisting of fish, eggs and bacon, rounded off with apple dumpling.

Can you beat that?—and we on our way to war.

The only thing required to make this repast perfect was a smoke, which was not forthcoming. In the early days the lack of good smokable cigarettes constituted one of the greatest hardships of the War.

On we travelled with never a stop, the morning getting hotter and the compartment in which we were huddled becoming more uncomfortable with each succeeding minute, due, for one thing, overcrowding, and to another, from causes mentioned in the preceding chapter, until eventually, at about noon, we halted and were shunted into a siding.

Our frantic efforts to get out were arrested by a peremptory command to remain where we were until further orders. We craned our necks out of the carriage window to view our surroundings.

A little way ahead of us was a small town.

At the side of us was a large tract of agricultural ground, being tended by a number of women and girls.

When the train first appeared on the scene, these workers contented themselves with a casual glance at it, and went on with their work. When, however, the officers descended from it, their interest was decidedly claimed, and their astonished gaze concentrated on the newcomers.

With a wild shriek they with one accord suddenly threw down their implements, and fled helter skelter towards the town.

What on earth was wrong with them? We asked one another. They were not performing in the manner our small experience had led us to expect. That something was decidedly amiss, was very evident.

The fearsome suggestion was muted, that somehow or other the train had lost its bearings during the night, and had run us into the middle of Germany. Such was our knowledge of the geography of Europe. The conduct of these extraordinary females bore this theory out, for we knew that French girls never by any chance run *away* from soldiers.

After a short consultation, three of our officers left the siding and proceeded into the town adopting, in our opinion, a rather furtive manner of progress.

Here was a fine mess, thought we. The pick of the British army lost in this careless fashion.

The re-appearance of one of these officers returning alone, brought our excitement to fever pitch.

'Ah,' almost sobbed the 'Pedler', 'the other two poor blighters "done in" before we've seen a shot fired.'

An order to detrain cut short our fevered speculations, and we made haste to obey, casting apprehensive glances around for a sight of the enemy.

'What chance do we stand with this blinking thing?' grumbled one of the lads, eyeing his stretcher malevolently.

'A "biery" one' cackled 'Pedler', and so it went on until our company commander, becoming aware of the delusion under which we were suffering, told us, with a silly grin, that in all possibility weeks would pass before we would smell a German, and then he would be quite a way off.

We accepted this rally with a comic mixture of relief and disappointment, which turned into feelings of the liveliest expectations, when he imparted to us the information that we were to be billeted in the town, which we could see ahead, named Taisnieres, for the next few days.

We marched from the siding and approached the town. As we advanced we beheld the inhabitants thronging out to meet us, and when we had drawn together, they made up to us for their previous aloofness.

We ascertained the cause of this unusual behaviour. It appears that when the train drew up and disgorged soldiers in a foreign uniform, the good field-workers jumped, in their excusable ignorance, to the conclusion that we could be nothing but the troops of the enemy, Hence their reason for going while the going was pretty sound.

Their flight into the town, during which they spread their unfounded fears in no uncertain manner, sucseeded in scaring everybody stiff, especially as they were practically undefended, most of their able-bodied men being away with the French Army.

The appearance of our officers in the town to pay their compliments, and to arrange accomodation, soon changed their fears into sensations of joy and satisfaction.

Our entry, consequently, was an epic of triumph, reaching its apex when we wheeled on to the square in front of the Mairie. Arrived here, a good deal of time was necessarily utilised in removing from our ranks a sufficient number of the populace to enable us to make some sort of a show of order. Having finally been arranged in as martial a manner as possible under the circumstances, we impatiently awaited the next moves in the game.

The First Act opened with a procession of sombrely clad dignitaries issuing from the Mairie.

They were headed by an aged, benevolent-looking old gentleman, wearing a tri-coloured sash about his middle, and a wonderful hirsute cultivation upon his face.

This worthy gentleman was the Maire.

Our Commanding Officer stood in front of his battalion slightly ahead of the remainder of the officers, waiting politely to receive him.

The Maire advanced steadily upon the Colonel until he arrived within striking distance, there he, to our great joy, threw his arms wildly around our respected commander's neck, and proceeded, apparently, to weep copious tears on each of his shoulders alternately.

Recovering from his supposed lachrymatory indulgences, he pulled himself together, and tore himself reluctantly away. Stepping back, his eye caught sight of the other officers as they stood, almost overcome by the terror of anticipation, behind the Commanding Officer.

The Maire's face brightened, for here was more good work awaiting him, and he gaily approached them, and subjected them to the same fate. Grinning with delighted amusement at this unique entertainment, I turned around to 'Pedler', who, to my surprise, was wearing a look of utter despair.

'What's biting you?' I asked him.

'Nothing at the moment, but from the look of things, something damned soon will be,' he replied. 'Take a peep at the savage old blighter now.'

I complied, and my merriment evaporated with great speed, for the old boy was standing out in front of the battalion, surveying us with an amorous look.

Apparently discovering among the thousand odd of us several fearsome faces that even he could not bring himself to cuddle, he turned away with a shrug of disappointed resignation, and, amid a great sigh of heartfelt relief from the men of the battalion, rejoined his colleagues.

The curtain now rose on Act II, revealing to our delighted gaze a full beauty chorus, led by a dainty 'Star' emerging from the portals of that Mairie.

Each bore a bouquet of wonderful flowers, and was attired in raiment of startling hue.

Their robes, we ascertained on closer acquaintance, were made of colours designed to represent the flags of the various Allies, and a truly weird conception they had of them, too. One, that after the tri-colour of France was most predominant, we guessed was intended to carry out the local idea of the banner of Britain.

The design consisted of a glaring red ground with a pale pink and blue mess hovering about in a corner. However, we let them get away with that on account of the other charms they displayed.

This bevy of delight demurely approached the Colonel, the chorus stopping a few feet from him, while the 'leading lady', with gracious carriage, swept on.

Arriving before the Colonel, she handed him her bouquet with a sweet smile, and dipped into a charming curtsy, and then drew herself proudly erect, facing him with a look of delicious expectancy.

He acknowledged her gift with a military salute. Much too military.

Still the girl stood waiting while a frown of perplexity formed on her brow.

A deep groan of sympathy for that poor child escaped us. 'Hell's Bell's' breathed 'Pedler,' 'can't the " old man" see that he ain't completed that job properly, according to their ideas, dekko, that poor fairy being disappointed through sheer ignorance.'

Any one of us, in the enviable position of the lucky recipient of these pleasing attentions, would have known exactly how to conclude the ceremony to the little lady's satisfaction. However, obviously unaware of his serious omission, the Commanding Officer turned to the Maire, and amid the compassionate sighs of the onlookers, both civil and military, the heartbroken girl crept crestfallen away.

The chorus, no doubt, fervently praying that they would have better fortune, now approached the other officers, and coyly presented each with a bouquet, watched by the jealous eyes of the 'other ranks.'

Unbelievable though it may seem, those dumb officers, with the presentation of such a glorious opportunity of emulating our old whiskery friend in his little cuddling act, on far, far, more pleasant subjects, simply smirked, and bobbed about a bit like a lot of cheerful idiots, and let it go at that. The girls stood looking at them, apparently petrified by amazement at their awful display of ignorance, and, attempting to shake off the horror and gloom that had descended upon them, they vanished dejectedly into the darkness of the Mairie.

'Knock me for a row of pie-cans,' implored 'Pedler,' 'those bloody fools ought to be employed guarding harems.'

A sudden stir among the lines drew our attention to the fact that the girls were about to stage another 'turn,' in spite of the 'bird' they had just received.

This time they appeared carrying baskets heaped up with loose blooms.

Someone suggested that the girls, being determined to obtain their just reward for their services, had decided to give those poor benighted officers another chance, in the forlorn hope that they would amend their behaviour.

To our unbounded joy, however, we observed them sweep haughtily past the wretched officers, and approach the humble rankers. Strolling slowly along

D

the ranks, they presented each man with a flower, and here the fun started.

Each bloom, as it was presented, was well and truly paid for, to the vast satisfaction of the recipient and the fair donor. Gone now was their previous air of depression, for had they not found at last that *some* Britishers at least were real men who knew exactly how to conduct themselves properly as demanded by such an important ceremony?

Whilst I was engaged in paying for several flowers, I became aware of bunches of bulging, staring eyes, turned in my direction, almost bursting with an envy, awful to contemplate.

They were the property of unfortunate members of the front rank, who, owing to their exposed position, and the proximity of the officers, had let slip their chance of showing their appreciation of the situation, through excessive timidity, thus affording an illustration of that proverb, 'a faint heart never pushed a perambulator.'

A cloud of giggling, blushing, and somewhat dishevelled beauties, issuing from the rear of the battalion, denoted that the fair side of the welcoming committee of Taisnieres had concluded the business they had so ably performed.

The murmurs of approval that arose from the spectators on the appearance of the girls, showed conclusively, that the inexplicable conduct of the officers had been atoned for by the gallantry of the men, and duly forgiven, and the *Entente* was once more restored to a firm footing.

The next item on the programme almost fell flat, as each of the members of the civilian deputation insisted on saying a little piece in a language we could not understand.

As the orations continued, however, an oft-recurring word used by all these speakers, attracted our wandering attention, especially as every time it was mentioned it occasioned a hearty expectorating contest among the French, and was accompanied by a comprehensive gesture, which consisted of drawing the hand, with the thumb pointing inwards, violently across the throat in a gruesome and highly suggestive manner.

The word sounded remarkably like 'bosh.'

We couldn't understand the reason for all this emotion at first.

We could only hazard a conjecture that whoever this guy 'bosh' was, he was absolutely vile and unspeakable, and it was perfectly clear that if he had the misfortune to fall into the hands of the fathers of Taisnieres he would receive very short shrift. A bright and intelligent lad at last found the clue. 'That word "bosh" is what these French blokes calls the Germans,' he ventured. Inquiries soon established the truth of this. 'Boche' was the term used by the French when referring to their hated enemy.

Possessed of this knowledge, the harangue assumed an interest. We breathlessly awaited the delivery of the despised word, and on it being pronounced, we supported our Allies in the throat-tickling act, with great gusto; an action very favourably received and noted by them, and which served to forge the links of admiration and friendship still firmer.

The citizens, having at last worn themselves completely out, retired, whereupon our commanding officer dismissed us to seek our billets, with a few fatherly words of warning and advice.

CHAPTER IV

Each company followed a guide, who led them to the quarters they were to occupy during their sojourn in the town.

My party, being the medical branch of the outfit, were allotted a billet apart from the remainder of the company, and our journey eventually finished up in front of a rickety barn, adjoining a promising-looking building. This barn was minus a door, and quite a good portion of its ceiling. On the wall outside was chalked the legend, '10 Hommes.'

With an air that one would expect the master of the Mint would assume when displaying his treasures, our guide invited us to step in and view this very undesirable and airy residence. Murmuring his felicitations on our good fortune in obtaining such a home, he handed it over to us, and took his departure.

'Where does the 10 homes come in' queriously inquired one of the men, 'there ain't enough of this to make one; all I can say is, the other ten families must be damned thankful we have turned them out.'

'You take another look round, my friend, and you will discover that the eviction of the former inhabitants has still to be proceeded with,' I pointed out.

Indeed a veritable riot was in progress in the darkness of the barn now we had entered, our appearance being greeted by a lively chorus of animal sounds, registering distinct anger and annoyance.

A herd of little pigs gambolling about two old sows, some cows and dozens of farmyard fowl, and a various assortment of other animals, strenuously contested our right of admittance, and they were only got rid of after a hot and lengthy engagement.

This skirmish having been brought to a successful conclusion, we set to work with grim determination to make the best of a bad job, and soon had the place looking as neat and tidy as the only hair on a bald man's head.

We festooned the walls with our equipment, hanging it about on improvised pegs, and commandeered some clean straw to serve us as beds.

This we spread about in selected places, the operation being accompanied by the hissing noises beloved of ostlers, and with many objurgations to imaginary steeds to 'git over' or 'hold up'. Our complacency was now seriously disturbed by the intelligence that an additional lodger, in the shape of a particularly un-popular sergeant, was to share our little home.

We next devoted ourselves to the cleansing and smartening up of our uniforms, etc., and having performed our ablutions we set forth to view the town.

I went along, accompanied by 'Pedler', and our pre-liminary discovery that the building, of which our billet was an outcrop as it were, was an estaminet, the local term for a 'pub', afforded us intense gratifi-cation.

This was of very short duration, for we were doomed to very bitter disappointment.

Among the orders issued for the guidance of the battalion was one that caused quite a great deal of heart burning, for it conveyed to us the painful intelligence that all 'pubs' were forthwith placed 'out of bounds.'

As far as the majority of the troops were concerned this order was superfluous, as very few possessed any money, no payments having been made since three or four days before leaving England. Those that did have cash were not overwhelmed with it, and contended successfully with the canniest native of the country north of the Tweed when it came to the question of parting with it.

A certain amount of consolation attended the thought that we were better off than most of our comrades, in so far as we were billeted in an edifice at least adjoining premises storing what 'Pedler' named, appropriately under the circumstances, 'near beer'. 'Pedler' and I considered the prohibition order unwarranted, and we concentrated on the search for a fairly safe means of circumventing it.

A thought striking us simultaneously, we turned and scuttled back into our billet, and subjected it to a close examination. The investigation showed us that all the walls were constructed of mud and laths, with the exception of the party wall that divided our billet from the estaminet, which was built of ordinary brickwork, making our intention to bore a hole through it a bit too tough a job.

' "So near and yet so far," fits this case admirably,' I said, as we leant longingly against the wall.

We next focussed our attention on the exterior.

The front of the estaminet with our quarters adjoining lay facing and parallel to the road.

At the rear were three other buildings, arranged so as to form a square.

In the centre of the square was a slimy and uninviting pond, in which some none-too-particular ducks disported themselves, flanked by an unsightly and unpleasant smelling heap of farmyard refuse, from which the pigs noisily selected tasty tit-bits, and the cow browsed daintily.

This caused 'Pedler' to entertain a troubled idea that the cow was being deliberately fed on this strong diet to acquire the smell and flavour to its milk necessary for it to be successfully converted into prime Limburger.

Our most important discovery was a roomy window on the ground floor at the rear of the estaminet, within six inches of the party wall.

Retiring into the barn we carefully excavated a small hole through its mud wall at the point where it adjoined the brick partition.

This hole was made just large enough to allow an arm to be comfortably passed through to the vicinity of the window. The completion of this operation laid the foundations of a scheme whereby we hoped to be able, later on, to get around the order that had been the cause of this activity on our part, and of so much perturbation generally.

Carefully concealing our handiwork with pieces of sackcloth, we proceeded with our delayed tour of inspection of the town.

We most particularly desired to find a shop in which we could secure some cigarettes, for we desired a 'smoke' above all other requirements. We had no knowledge of the language, and expected to encounter a little difficulty in making known our wants, but we guessed that a little judicious use of comprehensive actions would meet the case, and, full of confidence, we entered the first promising-looking store, and got busy.

After a great deal of futile pantomiming on both sides of the counter, which reduced us to the point of desperation and despair, we were about to give up and retire in defeat when the buxom and harassed proprietress, with the resigned air of a dying martyr, gave a last guess by way of a forlorn hope and murmured, 'cigarettes'?

She had solved our difficulty in that one little word, but how were we to know that she spoke 'English'?

This discovery pleased us immensely, and we rapidly fired several questions at her, but, apparently, her capabilities as an English linguist only extended as far as that one word. In payment for a couple of packets I placed a half a crown on the counter.

The good lady subjected it to a curious and careful scrutiny, at the end of which she shook her head dubiously. Glancing out of the door she suddenly sprang around the counter and dashed out of the shop, reappearing within a few moments, dragging with her one of the official interpreters attached for duty with the battalion.

After a very voluble flow of language, the extraordinary speed of which left us dizzy and gasping with amazement, he satisfied her that my money was quite good. A rate of exchange having been agreed on, she handed me a glittering heap of coins and a couple of packets of cigarettes. We both stood looking at the cash I had received from her, in bewilderment, as it lay in my hand with the opulent appearance of a pile of silver. I turned to the interpreter with a query, and on receiving his assurance that all was well, pocketed it without more ado, with a sensation of being in the possession of great wealth.

'Blimey,' muttered 'Pedler,' 'this is a real knockout. You put down half a crown and get a pound change in silver. If you've got any more, change them over quick.'

It did not take me long to ascertain that all French coins that glitter are not necessarily silver, and, moreover, on working the deal out, I made the rueful discovery that the lady had not treated me as generously as she might have done, for she had reckoned my two and sixpence as a two-shilling piece.

With hearty congratulations all around, we left the shop with an entirely mistaken idea that we had done remarkably well. Arriving outside, 'Pedler' hastily lighted his cigarette, and inhaled luxuriously, and I was about to follow suit, when my ear was almost shattered by an awe-inspiring bellow, followed by terrifying sounds of coughing and choking.

Turning hastily in surprise, I beheld 'Pedler' writhing and gasping apparently in the throes of a fearful agony, punctuated occasionally, when opportunity and sufficient breath permitted, by noises that sounded suspiciously profane.

'What's wrong? Pedler, old man,' I implored.

'Suffering nits. I'm nearly suffocated and poisoned,' was the only information he vouchsafed.

Highly puzzled by this unexpected outbreak, I thoughtfully lit up my own cigarette. At this action, I became acutely aware that any further explanation from him was unnecessary.

'I'm damned sure we can't possibly strike anything worse than these "fags" in this War,' mused 'Pedler.' 'I thought that my chance of going about chucking a chestful of medals had gone west,'

I have experimented with all kinds of material in an endeavour to ascertain their possibilities as a 'smoke.' In the days of my extreme youth I had tried out some of those little red Chinese crackers, that were the joy of every schoolboy in pre-war days, sheets of brown paper, and had even made one disastrous attempt at a home-made cigarette, manufactured of the discarded 'dottles' from powerful pipes, wrapped in newspaper, but, as poisonous as they proved to be, they were all infinitely preferable to these French outrages obtained in Taisnieres.

On our health improving as much as could be expected after undergoing such an ordeal, we moved sorrowfully away, leaving the vile cigarettes lying in the road where we had cast them in disgust. On second thoughts, however, we returned and retrieved them, and revolving in our minds several dark plots, in which the cigarettes figured prominently, we repaired us to our billet to convalesce awhile. On our way we spotted, with great glee, a potential victim of our deep-laid schemes, approaching.

He was a member of that fraternity, met with everywhere, whose chief claim to notice is a remarkable and clever ability in the art of obtaining all the good things of life, free. In other words, he was a highly successful 'mineser.'

We carefully baited our trap, placing in our mouths a cigarette, almost needless to mention, unlighted, and awaited his usual tactics. 'Whatcher, me old townies, 'ow goes it?' greeted he.

Then, staging a puzzled and concerned look, continued *sotto voce*, fumbling unceasingly in his various pockets, and behind his roomy ears, 'Nar, what's 'appened to those blinkin' things, then? What a mug; must 'ave gorn and left 'em in me bleedin' pack, and me wiv all that lot, too'; then addressing us direct, he continued, 'I was agoin' to offer you blokes a garsper, but I must 'ave left 'em in me kit be'ind.'

'Yes, you have, and a hell of a long way behind,' interrupted Pedler, rudely. 'For Jay's sake, dry up your tears, and take what you are asking for; I'll bet it will cure your craving for cigarettes for some time, especially "freemans".'

Handing him one of the infamous cigarettes, we hurriedly withdrew from him, as he, not one wit abashed by 'Pedler's' caustic remarks, joyfully applied a light, to his acquisition.

Looking back we saw that merchant gazing at his cigarette with a look of pained surprise.

On entering our billet to seek the repose necessary to enable us to recuperate from the effects of our fumigatory trials, we found that the remainder of the party were all out, and that their places had been amply occupied by the wretched farmyard stock we had, with so much pains, previously ejected.

Taking advantage of our absence, they had carried out a raid which had successfully restored them to their original habitation. What chaos they had produced in the quarters that we had so industriously made spic-and-span!

Pigs grunted their defiance at us, while chickens filled the air with their derisive and triumphant cacklings.

An old cow stood looking a pathetic picture of absolute boredom, while she slowly disposed of the last mouthful of my bed. An aged and decrepit old roué of a donkey, possessed of only one blasé eye, which he fixed on us disdainfully, leaned carelessly, with an air of utmost abandon and indifference, against the billet wall, ruminating on the doubtful flavour of a lump of the material torn from 'Pedler's' haversack.

A wild mêlée ensued, which resulted in the invaders being driven from the position, and we worked hard repairing the ravages our struggle had caused, and eventually arranged things more or less shipshape once again.

New straw was procured and spread over my part of
the floor, and 'Pedler' once more became the possessor
of a sound haversack, by the execution of the simple
operation of exchanging his damaged one with that of
the unpopular sergeant who had been swished upon us.
Throwing ourselves down with sighs of languor, we
shut our pretty blue eyes in preparation of slumber.
'Pedler' suddenly interrupted the atmosphere of calm
by springing up with a bloodcurdling curse, fondling
the back of his head gingerly at the same time. As he
drew his hand away I was horrified to see what I
imagined in the dim light to be great masses of blood
dripping from it. I was considerably relieved by the
results of an anxious inspection, which showed the
mess to be the remains of an egg, which a dear little
hen, acting with misplaced confidence in 'Pedler's'
gentle mien, had placed for him to hatch, by proxy,
as it were.

He made an awful pother about it, and I pointed out
to him at the time the action of the hen was no doubt
prompted by a desire to propitiate such a good-looking
young fellow as he was, but it took a long time before
his remarks upon the subject abated sufficiently to
enable me to sleep.

I was rudely aroused by some clumsy galoot step-
dancing on my face, and I was about to express the
adjectived opinion that it was quite frightful enough
as it was, without any additional mauling, when I
became aware of another uproar that was making good
progress. The sergeant was making awful strangled
noises, which I gathered had some little bearing on his

sudden discovery of the damaged haversack hanging on his equipment.

He drew us around him, and demanded, with fierce threats, the immediate surrender of the culprit responsible.

I examined the wreck gravely, with a convincing air of viewing it for the first time, and then ventured a studied opinion that the mice had been at it.

'Mice, you blooming idiot,' he bellowed in wrath, 'the mouse that could do that amount of damage would need to be as big as a horse.'

'Perhaps you're not far wrong,' I said drily, which was as much satisfaction as he could obtain, and we retired from his vicinity before he burst with outraged emotion.

The remainder of us simultaneously became aware that our own haversacks were crying for a little attention, which we hastened to give them, and the next few minutes were devoted to ostentatiously marking this useful article of equipment heavily with our names.

Our precautionary measures were interrupted by the announcement that 'tea' was ready.

What really happened was, the man who had been nominated "cook" merely for the reason, that of all soldiers in the army, he happened to possess the least qualifications for the job, banged a couple of 'Dixie' lids together and invited us to come and get 'it'.

'It', maybe—but never, by any stretch of the imagination, tea. 'Hell's brew' was not within miles of the same street, as the frightfulness of this concoction, which was a tepid, black, viscous mess, possessing a taste I should expect to find in a sample of water from a sewer. The lad was, undoubtedly, a tar boiler before he inflicted himself on the army.

Consoling myself with the thought that all these things are sent to try us, I did my best with it, sincerely hoping that better things were in store.

My little hope was to be realised, for, staggering away somewhat dazed after wrapping ourselves around some of that cook's concoction, the attention of 'Pedler' and I was engaged by the sight of groups of soldiers eagerly discussing some apparently incredible communication that had been imparted to them.

Drawing closer, we observed that a frenzied-looking sergeant flitted from group to group, haranguing them on a subject that, obviously, was the cause of amused pity and contempt.

Judging from the main burden of the men's remarks, we gathered that if that sergeant had acted on the bountiful advice freely offered him, the marines would have been kept busy doing their tale absorbing stuff until the crack of doom.

'Trying to sell something, Sergeant?' I artlessly queried as I joined a group.

'Sell something!' he iterated with a fine show of disgust, 'let me inform you that the only reason you cod-fish have heads is to save barbers from dying of starvation. Here am I, shouting myself hoarse, trying to get you to understand that on the market-square in front of the Mairie there are half a dozen barrels of beer, all free and to be had for the asking, and you receive the good tidings like a lot of hopeless idiots.'

'Don't be so funny, Dan Leno,' 'Put a sock in that and try another,' and other derisive remarks greeted his impassioned outburst, which exasperated him to such an extent that he ground out between his clenched teeth a rude imprecation, and with an 'I'm damned if I don't make you go', ordered us to 'fall in' forthwith, and marched us away to prove for ourselves the truth of his wild allegations. By all that was wonderful it was true. Neatly arranged at intervals on the square were eight barrels, each surrounded by a small group actively engaged in swallowing the contents. With a whoop we joined in, and made the welkin ring with loud gurglings and the smacking of appreciative lips. Either these sounds of unalloyed bliss or the smell of hops soon circulated over a large area, which resulted in the unwelcome appearance of reinforcements from all routes leading to the square. Soon the only indications remaining that barrels of beer were there were the heaps of struggling and gasping men that blotted them from sight.

Order and decorum were established by the efforts of the officers, assisted ably by the non-commissioned officers, and eventually each barrel sat perched in the centre of eight comparatively equal groups of admirers looking for all the world like little 'Queens of May' holding court in the midst of their retinue.

A nudge from 'Pedler' drew my attention to a bunch of old soldiers who had the reputation of being able to put away more beer than anybody had yet been able

E

to pay for. They were moving from barrel to barrel, earnestly subjecting the adherents of each to a careful scrutiny.

'Blimey, those blokes want watching; they look as though they're weighing up the chances of being able to click a barrel all to themselves,' whispered 'Pedler'.

'No. I've got an idea that they're looking around to see which group has the least number of "big capacity" boozers among them,' I replied.

Eventually selecting a group that apparently offered them the best opportunity of being able to secure the greatest amount of drink to themselves, they settled down among it, and I suggested to 'Pedler' that it would probably be a sound idea to benefit by the results of their observations and join them.

After a time both 'Pedler' and I were agreed that my diagnosis had been correct, and that our timely move had been wise, for the majority of the crowd we had favoured by our presence were well on the way to a condition that would effectually place them beyond the temptations of our barrel.

Musical instruments, much in favour with the 'Tommies' of those days, were mysteriously produced, and several jolly orchestras, made up of concertinas, accordians, mouth organs, etc., were formed, creating an atmosphere that made that square closely resemble Happy Hampstead on August Bank Holiday, especially when the least bashful of the men danced abandonedly with ladies they had extracted from among the inhabitants who thronged around in an admiring crowd and exchanged headgear with their fair partners, in the approved manner.

Songs that ranged from the canteen ballad concerning a ball-bearing naval rating, to the sentimental outpouring about a bird in a gilded 'cige,' were sung with much fervour.

Our French audience, although, of course, not understanding the words and meaning of the songs, which I am sure was quite a good thing for them, enjoyed our vocal efforts tremendously, and by their unstinted and vigorous applause urged us on to even more amazing feats in the song category.

During a slight lull in our uproar, a weird melody was heard emanating from a group of our French friends. There was a haunting familiarity about the air which puzzled us, and for a time defied all our efforts to identify it, but after a time it was borne upon us that our Allies were attempting to render us great honour by making this noise, that sounded like the outpourings of a herd of feline promenaders, in representation of our National Anthem.

Not to be outdone in this exhibition of love and goodfellowship, some of the boys responded with a rendering of their conception of the 'Marseillaise.'

As this outbreak assaulted them, the Frenchmen gazed at each other aghast with expressions of the greatest terror and pained surprise, as though inquiring of each other the nature of the offence they had committed that we should inflict this awful torture upon them. I doubt very much whether they ever recognised it for what it was intended to represent, but as I saw them eventually assume expressions of terrified admiration and awe, I gathered they had reached the conclusion that this savage row was an exhibition of our war-cry, and consoled themselves with the reflection that if later on it succeeded in scaring the Germans only half as badly as it had them, it was up to them, for the sake of the beloved 'La Patrie,' to bear the sacrifice entailed, of their loss of sleep for many a night to follow, and pretend to like it.

It was getting late, and instructions were given to close the festivities, which were carried out quite willingly, as each individual man had already assured himself, by a minute and solemn personal investigation, that the barrels no longer contained sufficient moisture to damp the throat of a gnat.

Solemn preparations were made to leave the scene of our *al fresco* smoking concert, and retire to a healing and much-needed sleep. The picture of the order of our parting from our French friends is faithfully reproduced every night outside of any London 'pub', after closing time, and gave many of us a strong reminder of home.

We clustered unsteadily around the inhabitants of the town, swearing iterated and maudlin oaths of eternal friendship, to the time-honoured strains of that dear old song, 'Dear old pals'.

Arrived safely back in our billet, the location of which, for some reason, we had great difficulty in discovering, we discussed the events of the day, and before surrendering ourselves to the soothing balm of sleep, we reached the unanimous conclusion that war was a fine thing, and that people that wrote or spoke the contrary, either didn't know what they were talking about or were liars.

The credit of providing this entirely unexpected treat belongs to our officers, a jolly considerate lot of gentlemen, who, knowing of the straitened financial condition of the men, clubbed together and provided us with an excellent and well-appreciated entertainment.

CHAPTER V

THE next morning a series of grunts and snuffling sounds aroused me from my heavy slumber, and I lay awhile idly wondering what ailed the sergeant's voice this morning. Maybe he had been greedy the night before, and was now suffering the penalty demanded for over-indulgence in the cup that cheers.

Realising that the sounds I heard, while bearing a distant resemblance to the sergeant's usual way of expressing himself, possessed a subtle difference, I jerked myself fully awake, and found that the disturbers of my peace were half a dozen of those quadrupeds, that, when they have crossed the bourne to their happy hunting-grounds, become known under the synonym of pork.

They were engaged in a determined effort to uproot the barricade that did duty as a door to our billet, noisily telling each other during the process of the terrible amount of damage they would create once they got inside.

Dawn had just broken, and the activities of these little brutes, who were far too early by hours with the production of their 'reveille' act, roused my keen resentment.

I arose wearily, and, eliciting a number of unfriendly expressions of ill will from a hard-bitten veteran, in whose ear I had, inadvertently, caught my toe, proceeded to do some cruel stuff to those pigs, in the hope of inducing them to suspend their operations about the barn, and retire.

Believing I had successfully taught them the lesson that to rob good soldiers of their hard-earned sleep was a thing simply not done, I 'returned to my couch.

I had no sooner settled myself down comfortably again, when they returned to the attack, with renewed vigour, and a greatly augmented tumult of defiant grunts and snorts.

To make matters appertaining to peaceful rest impossible, the other denizens of the farm now decided to take a hand in the game, and, rendering able service in support of the confounded pigs, effectually banished from us all ideas of further slumber that we may have entertained that morning.

Rising sore and disgruntled at our early awakening, we busied ourselves with cleaning-up and making thoroughly tidy the billet and our persons.

These offices completed, 'Pedler' and I went out for a constitutional walk.

Strolling across some fields, we discovered some very excellent mushrooms, of which we collected, between us, about fifty, which we pleasurably anticipated relishing with our otherwise tasteless breakfast.

Seeking out our company cook with great stealth, possessing for some inexplicable reason a confidence in his ability to do us and our find justice, we tempted him to enter into a conspiracy with us, promising him, as a reward, an equal share in our mushrooms, for which, in return, he was to provide us with a highly succulent breakfast.

Alas! for our expectations. I certainly had enough experience of the capabilities of that cook to prevent me from entrusting to his tender mercies such an important and delicate culinary task, and in acting against my better judgment in invoking his assistance, I fully deserved the results.

Although we had handed to him the whole of the fifty odd mushrooms, when he had placed our breakfast before us, we failed to identify anything remotely resembling one.

The mess in front of us looked suspiciously like the front portion of a dirty old tunic he was wont to wear when about his greasy occupation, after it had fallen foul of the fire.

It was a charred streak of unappetising-looking material, adorned by three or four sorry objects, appearing very much like burnt buttons.

This mess he expected us to swallow as fried rashers of bacon and mushrooms.

We were rendered absolutely speechless; not that that state of strangled verbosity mattered in the least, for all the words in the world would not have been sufficient to enable us to express even a hint of our feelings on the subject, or of our opinion of that 'cook.'

He occasioned me so much dire misery and constant pain, that I began to brood and weigh up the successful chances of various murderous schemes I contemplated with a view to ridding myself, once and for all, of these evil machinations, called by him, in his sublime ignorance, cooking. Every man is entitled to his own opinion, poor brute.

Breakfast over, the men were all warned to parade. Instructions were received that one man was to be exempted per billet, for the purpose of remaining to guard the effects and belongings of the men, that had been necessarily left behind.

As I held the choice of selection, I permitted this onerous duty to devolve upon myself, and I later lounged tantalisingly against the front of our billet, and watched the remainder of the lads, with many an envious glance in my direction, march away to be unpleasantly subjected to hot and arduous exercises and manœuvres. After they had departed from my sight, I began to feel rather lonely, and found myself lacking something with which to occupy my mind and leisure.

I saw a bunch of girls and went over to them, and tried my hand, unsuccessfully, at practising a few gallantries, but failed to make any headway in this commendable direction at all. All my attempts to convey my regard for them, by subtle flatteries, and generally to be pleasant and agreeable, produced nothing more than idiotic smirks from them and from me.

The beauties and utility of a universal language now became forcibly apparent to me. I was confirmed in the belief that life could be considerably improved by such an innovation.

Reluctantly surrendering these vain ideas of passing away a pleasant hour or two in this desirable manner, I sought other diversions, and almost at once succeeded in finding one.

Returning to the neighbourhood of the billet, I had resumed my recumbent attitude in front of it, when my wandering attention became attracted by some peculiar sounds, the nature of which I, at first, was at a loss to define.

Patient concentration told me that they originated at some point in the rear of the billet, and it slowly penetrated into my understanding that these noises held a subdued note of appeal, which decided me to rake up enough energy to allow me to investigate. I strolled casually around to the back with this project in mind, and on arrival was rewarded by a most unusual sight.

Presented to my astonished gaze was (in those far-off days) the rare sight of a pair of shapely legs, obviously the property of a member of the fair sex, projecting upwards out of a round stonework building, which I at once realised was a well. The legs were energetically waving about, while pitiful sounds of distress, becoming momentarily more pronounced, drifted out from the depths of the well into the air.

I immediately grasped the startling fact that someone was in a more or less uncomfortable predicament which called for instant action, and I overcame any feelings of embarrassment the spectacle had roused in me, and hurriedly bridged the gap between us. Clutching the legs and closing the eyes smartly, I put in a few

minutes of hefty hauling, which finally resulted in the
recovery of the remainder of the body.

The victim of this unfortunate *contretemps* stood, very
dishevelled, blushing and panting fiercely, gazing at
me for a second or two, and then, in a sudden wild
burst of complete abandonment, threw her arms
around my neck and expressed her thanks and appreciation of my gallantry in a highly satisfactory manner
which recompensed me completely for the strain
the unexpected and not unpleasant sight of her
nice legs had inflicted upon my timid and shrinking
morals.

She was a buxom, rosy-cheeked, cheerful-looking
young woman, about twenty-five years old, and we
wasted quite a lot of time between us in mutual vocal
efforts, she, no doubt, trying to explain the cause of
the catastrophe, which was obvious, and her thanks
for my timely intervention, while I attempted to let
her know what exquisite pleasure the rescue had
afforded me.

The exercise of a little deduction explained to me the
reason she had adopted such an immodest attitude.
She had been leaning over the well, hauling up a
heavy bucket of water, when one of her feet slipped and
caused her to overbalance, head foremost, into it.
Fortunately she had retained her common sense, and
had immediately released her hold of the rope attached
to the bucket. She had thus been able to arrest her
descent into the murky depths beneath by obtaining
a precarious hold on the rough masonry of the interior.
There she remained lodged, afraid to move either

backwards or forwards less the movement should compel her to lose her grip, her only hope of rescue depending upon an answer to her muffled calls for assistance.

Her cries had failed to reach the ears of the inhabitants of the estaminet, as they were probably immersed in duties that took them out of earshot of her feeble attempts to attract their attention. This nice young woman now caught me by the arm, and guided me into the estaminet. This proceeding was, of course, against orders, but I did not offer undue resistance to this course, as, for one thing, there did not appear to be anyone in authority about who would be likely to interfere with me, and another, that a lapse on my part might conceivably be overlooked on such an occasion.

I was considerably abashed, therefore, on arriving inside, to find one of our officers sitting at a table, engaged in writing. He was a temporary inmate of the house, being billeted in a room of the premises.

This discovery upset my calculations, and I hastily made to retire, but he, apparently interested in something which the young woman I had assisted was very volubly explaining, arrested my retrograde movement, and bade me wait.

There were three other persons present, consisting of two women, one about sixty-five, the other about forty, and a boy about fifteen. My guide, having reached the end of her discourse, turned again in my direction, which apparently was a signal for the whole crowd to precipitate themselves upon me, which action they proceeded to carry out, striving amongst themselves for precedence in according me the honours they considered were my due for the service I had rendered.

That this scene afforded the officer almost as much pleasure as it did me, was evident by the expressions of mirth that chased themselves over his countenance.

When the general engagement had subsided into a little promiscuous sniping on the part of the youngest lady, the officer, who spoke French fluently, explained the reason for this overwhelming display of affection for me.

The young woman I had enjoyed the happiness of extracting from her awkward position, and untimely ablutions, was the old lady's only daughter, and the apple of her eye. The other woman was her daughter-in-law, whose husband was away doing duty with the French army, and the boy was the old lady's grandson.

'You appear to have made yourself pretty popular with these people, and they have asked me to tell you that anything they possess is yours for the asking,' he went on.

'Right, sir, if you have no objection, I would like to sample a little of their wine,' I ventured.

'I'll convey your desires to the lady, but don't overdo things and get yourself into trouble,' he said, and, passing on my request, he departed.

The old lady, beaming with good will and pleasure, now bustled in bearing a very promising-looking bottle, and some glasses, which she speedily filled.

Lifting a glass, with great anticipation, I awaited the others to follow suit, and we toasted each other with huge grins that amply expressed the good will that we could not orally convey.

I proposed to swallow the entire contents of the glass without a pause, but hurriedly altered my intention at the first mouthful. 'Ye Gods ! ' I muttered, an outbreak quickly smothered as I remembered my manners, and I continued with the thought that the old dame had produced a bottle of Condy's by mistake. That was certainly the startled impression I formed, on getting the taste of the drink she had provided.

I quickly scanned the company to see if they evinced any sign showing that they had observed something unusual about the drink, but I only met profound expressions of the utmost satisfaction. It was evident that they were very proud of this terrible concoction, and having no desire to offend against such well meant hospitality, I bravely swallowed both my repugnance and the horrid contents of my glass, feeling that the outcome was likely to savour more of the hospital than the hospitality. Honours being concluded, I took advantage of the very first opportunity that presented itself to steal away to the nearest convenient place where I surreptitiously rid my mouth of that vile flavour. Thus passed a Tommy's first introduction to Vin Rouge.

At about eleven o'clock I was sitting on the shaft of an old farm waggon that stood in the yard, ruminating and idly watching the amusing but slightly disgusting antics of several little pigs enjoying a feed. I couldn't understand why these animals considered it essential to wallow in the filthiest mess in their vicinity before paddling in the vessel containing their food.

I had just reached a conclusion that this operation rendered them the same service that the usual condiments did for us, when I observed the old lady beckoning me.

I politely went over to her, and she seized me, and propelled me inside her house, and sat me down at a table behind a very 'Owen Nares' of stews.

The remainder of the family took their places at the board, and for the next ten minutes only the sounds of mastication broke the silence.

More wine was proferred, but I found that I had suddenly developed a strong prohibition urge, anyhow as far as that wine was concerned. Once again I fancied I had a distinct grievance against the language barrier. I badly wanted to let them know that I pined for beer. Not being aware that I had only to mention the word to enable them to make me happy, I sadly pointed to the only thing possible in the way of drinks, and tried to successfully pretend that the only liquid able to bring me true satisfaction was water.

(You will understand from that how terrible that wine really must have been.)

This surprising demand filled them with astonishment, and they exchanged pitying glances with one another, accompanied, I have no doubt, by an almost overmastering desire to tap their heads with their fingers significantly, a movement restrained by their anxiety to make me feel at home, and their timely remembrance of their correct attitude as hostesses.

What a gorgeous feast that was.

The pleasant thought flitted across my mind that I was now independent of the administrations of that tar-boiling cook of ours, and it expressed itself in a happy grin that spread over my face, and infected my good friends to such an extent that we concluded the meal with much laughter.

Leaving the estaminet I returned to the billet just in time to greet 'Pedler' as he came in from parade.

He had undergone a gruelling time, and was very 'fed up', as he strongly expressed his state of mind.

'No more than I am,' I said, and in answer to the look of contempt directed at me at the passing of that frivolous remark, I told him of the manner in which I had managed to pass away the morning. He pleaded desperately with me, asking me to take him in immediately to introduce him the delights to be obtained in the estaminet. I resisted these appeals on the score that in acting so rashly we could not fail to attract undesirable attention, to the detriment of a little scheme that I had in mind by which I would be able to assist him in gaining his desires later on during the evening.

In the evening 'Pedler', refusing to accompany me, being sore and surly over my refusal to accede to his unreasonable request of earlier in the day, I wandered into the town alone.

F

The troops having completed their parades for the day, were out in the streets in force, ogling the belles of the village as they passed and repassed.

A scene strongly reminiscent of Wigan on a Sunday night. Whilst walking through the town at this time I experienced an encounter that changed the whole course of my life, whether for better or worse, I have never yet been able to make up my mind. I have mentioned in a previous chapter that I was the best shot of my company. As, however, I held certain qualifications of a medical nature, I was condemned to be a non-combatant. This rôle by no means met with my approval, and, strangely enough, I was thinking of this state of things, and wondering if there was any possible and satisfactory way out, when I was accosted by a corporal who had rejoined the regiment from the Reserve on the outbreak of the War.

He opened his conversation, remarking to me in tones of undisguised envy :

'You are a lucky fellow!'

'I've never found that I possessed that much-to-be-desired atmosphere,' I countered. 'What makes you think so?'

He replied, telling me that when he was on the Army Reserve, he joined a section of St. John Ambulance Brigade.

'I became very interested in the work,' he continued, 'and obtained almost every first aid certificate it was possible to acquire. Here am I now serving in the ranks, without a chance to put my knowledge to the best use, consequently all my training is going to be wasted, look at all these certificates!' and he handed me about a dozen of them. On examining them I found that they amply sustained his statements.

'Would you be willing to change duties with me?' I asked him.

'There is nothing I would like better,' he replied simply.

'Right you are! You come along with me, for I have an idea that the exchange can be arranged without any difficulty, to our mutual satisfaction,' I said.

I conducted him direct to the presence of my company commander, and explained the object of our visit. Ascertaining that we were unanimous in the desire to exchange, he expressed himself entirely in favour of the project, and promised to further it immediately. We left the company headquarters, and outside, after an exchange of mutual and hearty congratulations, we parted, he, no doubt, to ruminate on his 'good luck' and me to my billet nursing a feeling that this was my day out.

This poor devil was killed by one of the first shots fired against British troops in the War, in a most cowardly fashion, while gallantly leading his stretcher-bearing party to the succour of some of our badly-wounded casualties, on the morning of the twenty-third of August, 1914.

Darkness had fallen when I arrived back at the billet, and I sought 'Pedler,' and advised him to go inside the billet and take up a position in the proximity of the hole in the wall that we had made earlier on, and to

stand there, using the utmost caution to avoid attract-
ing undue attention, and to await further develop-
ments, which would be heralded by a signal from me.

Walking carefully to the back of the estaminet, I
peeped into the window, and was seen immediately by
my fair hostesses, who made a concerted charge upon
the door, which they hastily unbolted and admitted
me.

Inside, the old lady tried to convey to me some
little intelligence, which, although she was very ably
seconded in her efforts by the remainder of the family,
I failed to grasp.

Giving up her useless oral attempts with a shrug and
a friendly smile, she lit a candle, and signing to me
to follow, proceeded up some ricketty stairs.

These led up into a spacious chamber that occupied
the whole length and breadth of the building. It was
furnished, among other usual bedroom accessories,
with four huge beds.

Leading me to one of these beds, the old lady made
me understand, by the most unmistakable gestures,
that it would afford her the greatest pleasure if I would
honour her and her house by making use of it.

I did not hesitate to signify my acceptance. It was
the most comfortable-looking bed I had ever seen,
containing a huge old-fashioned box spring mattress,
and spread with linen like snow and enticingly
fragrant.

Beaming with pleasure, she escorted me back to the
living-room. I now considered it essential, if I was to
enjoy the comfort of that delightful-looking bed, to

obtain some sort of cover for my presence in the room, which was situated in proscribed area, as it were.   I therefore decided to take the bull by the horns, and, with a palpitating heart, I approached the door of the room occupied by my officer friend of the morning.

Entering in response to his invitation, I placed my dilemma before him, speaking fair in the following manner; 'Sir, you know of the little incident of this morning, wherein I was able to render to the inmates of this house some little service, and you are aware of their feelings toward me in consequence. They have ever since been trying to express their gratitude, almost to the point of embarrassment. A moment ago they caught me outside the billet, and seized me and dragged me in here, and then bolted the doors so that I should not be able to evade their expressions of kindness any longer. The old lady then led me upstairs, where she showed me a bed and made me——'

'Stop! good Lord! what the devil have you been up to,' he interrupted me surprisedly.

'Nothing, sir! I haven't finished what I intended to tell you,' I replied, hurt by his interruption.

'Continue, then, and let me have the worst,' he commanded resignedly.

'I was telling you that she made me understand that she would be grievously offended if I refused to take advantage of it; I should hate to appear rude to her, and it really is a nice-looking bed, but the difficulty lies in the fact that, as far as I am concerned, this building is "out of bounds," consequently I have no right to be here. May I ask you sir, what you would advise me to do about it?'

'Do! you idiot,' he bawled, 'just take my advice and make the most of that bed you can, it may be years before you get another opportunity to lie in a decent bed.'

'Then I have your permission to remain, sir?' I asked.

'Yes, and don't give me any more scares,' he barked, as I swiftly backed away.

Back in the living-room the ladies produced some bottles of wine. One of these I took, and walking over to the window, I opened it and gave a subdued whistle.

Immediately a clutching hand at the end of a snaky arm appeared as though by magic, and, almost as soon disappeared holding tightly the bottle of wine.

At first my peculiar action puzzled the good ladies, but perceiving my object, they eagerly supplied me with more to dispatch on the same journey.

I waited for a while before handing on the others, expecting each moment to hear a burst of violent abuse from 'Pedler' as he sampled the drink I had handed him, but as, to my surprise, nothing of the kind was heard, I signalled again, and the hand once more executed its amazing appearing and disappearing act, which left me marvelling at the depraved taste displayed by 'Pedler', a trait up to then, entirely unsuspected by me.

I tendered some money with the view of recompensing these people for the drink so unstintingly supplied, but they indignantly returned it to me.

Signing to me to take my place at the table, they surrounded me by a barrage of supper. Whilst actively engaged in encircling the good things before me I received evidence that I possessed a feeble mind.

One of the women, holding out a bottle of wine to me, sent out an interrogatory, 'Vin?' 'No?'

'No!' I replied with an air of finality.

She then said something with a questioning air, from among which the word 'beer' seemed to emerge.

Certain that it could not mean what I hoped it would, I nevertheless risked an affirmative nod, and within a few seconds I was agreeably astonished to find a large and healthy glass of beer at my elbow. It remained there for about one-thousandth part of a second, and that long simply because I was temporarily rendered incapable of movement by amazement.

'Nothing attempted, nothing done,' I mused, thinking, with regret, of the dumbness that had prevented me from obtaining such a refreshing drink that morning. True, I did not expect to find that the main difference between English and French beer was mainly the matter of an 'I'.

During the whole of this time, at frequent intervals, I kept 'Pedler' well supplied with wine, and other good things, and it soon became apparent that I had been doing him too well for his good, for, forsaking caution, he became noisy in his cups, and attracted the attention of the other inmates of the billet. In his turn, the sergeant was brought to life, and he, in a loud voice, immediately demanded to know the cause of the disturbance.

Upon hearing this baleful sound, I hurriedly closed the window, and withdrew from the scene, to my seat at the table. The atmosphere of calm was rudely disturbed by a violent hammering at the door, and a nasty voice vulgarly ordered me to come outside.

I affected to be deaf and dumb to these blandishments, and I continued to sit with a feeling that a pair of eyes were burning great holes in my back, as I critically held up, and examined a glass of beautifully clear amber-coloured liquid by the light of the lamp.

This innocent action appeared to rouse the interrupter to a pitch of frenzy, for he redoubled the volume of his infernal racket. At this, the officer's door flew open, and he streaked into the living-room.

'What the hell is happening?' he demanded angrily.

I explained that I thought that somebody was anxious to come in. Raging furiously, the officer unbolted the door, threw it open, and then told that sergeant a lot of things about himself that he had never suspected.

After this storm peace reigned once more, and on the boy lighting his candle and ascending to the upper regions, I signified my desire to follow suit, which met with approval, and before the passing of a few seconds I had divided the sheets of my wonderful bed. I dozed off idly speculating on the reason for the presence of the other beds.

A rustling and whispering drew me back from the verge of slumber, and on opening my eyes to see what it was all about, I received the jolt of my young life.

Across the room the three ladies, without regard for

the shock they were administering to my morals, were unconcernedly preparing for bed.

It may not have been anything out of the ordinary to them, but I had not been brought up that way, and it was with a sigh of distinct relief that I felt that the candles had been put out, and I was free to relieve my eyes of the strain I had imposed upon them, in trying to keep them, in my inordinate modesty, shut.

CHAPTER VI

THE following morning I awakened with a wonderful sensation of rested ease and well-being, having soundly slept the whole night round for the first time since war had been declared.

Stretching luxuriously in my comfortable bed, I caught sight of the time by my watch, and was considerably surprised to find that it had passed eight o'clock.

Gazing around the sleeping chamber, I was relieved to see that I was the sole occupant, and I hastily arose and attired myself, and descended to the regions below.

Proceeding to the well, I carefully drew up a supply of refreshingly cold water, and enjoyed a thorough wash, the only thing lacking to make it perfect being soap, which could not be procured in this part of France at any price. This inability to secure that most necessary adjunct to a successful cleansing, provoked a great deal of astonishment among us, especially as the inhabitants did not appear to suffer unduly in their appearance through the deficiency. Completing my ablutions, I returned into the estaminet, where I was supplied with a delicious breakfast of rolls, and most excellent coffee. Having concluded this refreshing repast, I took a stroll around to the billet.

On entering, I encountered the sergeant. I politely asked him if he had slept well, remarking that, as far as I was concerned, I had just passed the most comfortable and enjoyable night of my life. His answer was, to my surprise, very terse and rude, and caused me to entertain a suspicion that he did not like me.

I found 'Pedler' looking and feeling very sheepish; and when he assured me, in extenuation of his foolish and indiscreet conduct of the preceding night, that he had consumed at least four of the bottles of vin rouge, himself, alone and unaided, I fully grasped the reason. The fact that he had been able to accomplish that remarkable feat, and still remain alive, compelled my reluctant admiration, if it failed to arouse my sympathy.

Whilst in the act of explaining to 'Pedler' what a loss of good things his greediness had caused him to sustain, an interruption occurred, occasioned by the appearance in our billet of the St. John Ambulance man, my acquaintance of the evening before.

He bore an order, commanding me to hand over my duties and outfit to him, and to report myself to my company headquarters forthwith. The exchange of duties had been successfully effected, and consequently I was jubilant, until I became conscious of the fact that I had, by my action, rashly sacrificed my very pleasant board and lodging at the billet.

How I now vainly regretted my hastiness, but I realised that it was of no earthly use crying now that the milk was spilt, and I sorrowfully prepared, with a heavy heart, to carry out my instructions. Before leaving I repaired to the estaminet to bid a fond and sad farewell.

It required the discussion of quite a number of drinks to make my friends realise the awful fact that I was about to be brutally torn from them.

When at last the terrible calamity about to befall them did penetrate into their understanding, they exhibited great manifestations of grief and despair.

I went back again to the billet, and joined in another affecting scene, that took place between 'Pedler' and I.

'Cheer up, "Pedler," old boy, weep not so bitterly; be nice, and be sure you do everything your new corporal tells you, and if you are a good little boy I'll drop in and see you when I come back from the War,' I soothed him, but really, we were both frightfully upset, for it was the first time we had been parted for years. Reporting to my company, I was given command of a section that had been the original charge of the corporal with whom I had exchanged duties, and it did not take me very long to learn the vast difference that existed between the solidly comfortable job I had foolishly relinquished, and my new one, which seemed to be full of unaccustomed activities such as marching, skirmishing, and messing aimlessly about in general.

'Pedler' put in an appearance in the early part of the evening, and told me that the ladies had been mooning about since I had been away, like old cows looking for their young. I was inclined to resent this distinctly uncomplimentary manner of referring to my angels of mercy, but let it go on 'Pedler' assuring me that no insult had been intended, but that it was merely his unfortunate way of expressing himself.

He also wanted to know the strength of a rumour he had heard to the effect that we were to receive some pay, which I rather suspect was the real cause of his visit to me.

While we were engaged in this exchange of amenities, we were disturbed by a terrific cheering that resounded in the vicinity. On seeking the cause of this outburst, we found that 'Pedler's' rumour had become a positive fact, which is not the usual way of pleasant rumours. Pay parade was to be held at company headquarters at once, and we 'fell in' and lined up, and anxiously awaited the delivery of our emoluments, which were very badly needed. Each man duly received a dole of five francs, equivalent in value at that time to four shillings and twopence, English. Not a great amount, it is true, but very thankfully received by us, in those hard times.

At the conclusion of the pay parade, the officer-in-charge, cast a certain amount of gloom over the proceedings by asking each man if he had made out his will. This sounded extremely ominous, and conjured up decidedly unpleasant visions.

Those answering the question in the negative were called upon to give a reason for their abstinence from performing this uninspiring part of the war game. The majority of them put forward the excuse that they hadn't bothered for the very simple reason that they had nothing in the world to leave to anyone.

One bright fellow said: 'My old gal said sumfink ter

me abart it 'fore I left, but I told 'er that she needn't fret 'er fat; if I was agoing ter kick the bucket, I would do it "intesticle".'

On receiving our dismissal from the pay parade, 'Pedler' and I decided to take a walk out of the town and view the surroundings. We selected a road leading out from the town in a northerly direction, and were soon clear, and in the country beyond.

We had plodded along for some two miles, exchanging comments upon anything that appealed to our interest, and we were about to pass a large farm that was situated about a hundred yards from the entrance to a village, when our ears were suddenly assailed by sounds of girlish shrieks of delight, accompanied by manly exclamations of intense satisfaction.

The familiar tones of these remarks immediately claimed our attention, and caused 'Pedler' and I to look at each other in surprise. The words we had heard had been expressed in the inimitable language of the 'cockney.'

As we could not understand the reason for the presence of a native of London town in this locality, we decided to investigate the phenomenon, and we accordingly entered the precincts of the farm.

We found a large farm wagon, loaded with hay, standing at the edge of a newly-mown field. On the top of the hay stood three figures—an old woman, a comely and saucy-looking wench, and a humorous-looking young man, who, bareheaded and minus his coat, was vigorously pitching the hay from the wagon to a budding hay-rick, where it was received and evenly distributed by two old men.

The women stood by his side regarding his efforts with the greatest admiration.

As we were nearing the scene of these rustic activities the young man straightened himself, and, pausing from his labours, directed a swift glance at the girl. He next drew his bare arm across his mouth, seized her by the waist, and imprinted a hearty and somewhat boisterous kiss upon her rosy cheek. It was clear that the girl approved of his action, for she greeted it with a ringing peal of laughter, which was accompanied by the loud chuckles of her compatriots.

'Whatcher go on that one "Cherry"? "Tray bong?" ' we heard him ask in tones expressive of great satisfaction.

'Oui!' saucily answered the maiden, at which he again seized her, saying:

'Yer does, does yer! Well, 'ow abart this fer a better one?' and our envious eyes witnessed a repetition of the interesting operation.

'Well, I'm hanged! If that bloke ain't "Pinky White" of the "fuzzies" I'll eat me blooming kitbag," exploded 'Pedler'. He had named an old friend, a member of that distinguished regiment: The Royal Fusiliers.

'Bill, Oh! "Pinky," 'ere comes yer old woman,' bellowed 'Pedler.' At which 'Pinky' started violently and peered anxiously in our direction.

At the sight of us he, apparently, experience a great relief, for his erstwhile worried expression gave place to a huge grin, which threatened to envelop his ears, a catastrophe that was timely averted when the smile was arrested by his efforts to shout:

'Well! If it ain't a couple of me ole "Middy" pals. 'Ow goes it me ole " chinas"? Wot the 'ell are yer doin' 'ere?'

'We've just popped rahnd ter 'elp yer ter do a bit o' cortin' "Pinky",' replied 'Pedler'.

'Oh! did yer! Nuffink doin', me ole cock! She wouldn't as much as look at any one bar me,' bragged 'Pinky'.

'I believes yer, "Pinky". She's like the ole girl at the monkey 'ouse, 'orribly fascernated!' retorted 'Pedler', with a bitterness that, I fear, was generated by envy.

After a little more repartee 'Pinky' invited us to join him in his labours, an offer that we promptly accepted, but our ardour was considerably diminished when 'Pinky', by means of a series of extraordinary gesticulations, induced the girl to retire into the farmhouse.

The cart was speedily unloaded by our united efforts, and then 'Pinky' informed us that the farmer had asked him to invite us to partake of a little refreshment, as an acknowledgment of our good services. I do not know by what means 'Pinky' ascertained the farmer's desires in the matter, but, accepting his assurance that everything was in order, we entered the farmhouse.

With great audacity 'Pinky' assumed the rôle of host, and his comportment was that of a favoured member of the family; an attitude which obviously received the full support of the farmer and his wife.

F

During the course of the ensuing conversation, we learnt from 'Pinky' that he was the batman of an officer who was billeted at the farm, and that his regiment was quartered in the adjoining village.

Concluding a very pleasant evening, we retraced our steps to Taisnieres.'

The novelty of our surroundings was now beginning to pall on us, and we were again haunted by a disturbing impression that the War had either ended, or was about to be ended by the French Army, without our aid.

We could glean no news as to the progress of the War, being, to all intents and purposes, isolated from any sources of information, with the exception of local French newspapers, which we were unable to read.

With increasing gloom we continued each day to carry out the same old exercises, gradually losing all interest in them and the distant War, until signs that a change was probable became evident on the night of August 20th.

CHAPTER VII

Early on the morning of the twenty-first of August we received orders to prepare to leave Taisnieres at last.

All was bustle and excitement now that a move towards the real thing appeared imminent.

Baggage wagons were carefully overhauled, and inspections of all kit and equipment, etc., were held, and the articles subjected to a rigorous examination, until everyone was satisfied that we were prepared to meet any foe we might encounter, and we were ready to take the road.

Before parading I went around to a call on my French lady friends, and to bid them a final farewell.

Succumbing to their pitiful pleadings, I surrendered some of my shoulder titles and badges as souvenirs, and gave them one each. A sorry enough award for all their kindness to me during my sojourn in their home, but even these small brass decorations were highly coveted by the French of our acquaintance, and owing to the great demand made upon the men of the battalion for them, by fair souvenir-hunters, they had increased in value until, at this time, they were almost at a premium.

To them belonged the honour of being the sole recipients of tribute by me of this nature, to date.

In exchange, they pressed upon me a nice little alarm clock that I had, on several occasions during my short acquaintance with them, expressed my admiration for.

It was unique in its way, its chief claim to novelty being its method of giving the alarm. Its warning consisted of a silvery and very musical reproduction of an extract from a popular French opera.

We said our farewells, and parted very reluctantly, with a display of tears on the part of the ladies, especally by the old lady, who had, I believe, conceived quite a genuine regard for me, and I returned to my company, and placed their gift into my haversack. When we paraded, the whole town turned out to give us a rousing send-off. Here, again, we became the objects of a floral demonstration, women and girls presenting us with garlands of beautiful flowers, with which we decorated our rifles and ourselves.

At about ten o'clock in the morning we commenced our march from that town of many very pleasant memories, towards the unknown, proceeding on our way with the highest spirits to the martial and inspirating strains emitted by multifarious musical instruments operated by men of talent present in the unit.

A real martinet, at the sight of the battalion moving out from Taisnieres that day, would have been seized by frightful convulsions in attempting to reduce to coherent expression his opinion of the incongruity of it.

The scene partook more of the nature of a carnival procession than the grim march of men going to wage war.

Flowers and ribands streamed from the barrels of our rifles, and from every conceivable portion of our uniform, whilst swarms of giggling and shrieking girls and women weaved in and out of our ranks, presenting us with all manner of good things, such as chocolate, fruit and eggs, etc. Some of them even bore buckets of an intimate domestic nature which contained, on this occasion, beverage belonging to the category that is banned to misguided disciples of Bands of Hope.

The military aspect of the column improved as we travelled, and each kilometre pushed behind us saw a corresponding slackening in the display of fervour by our fair followers until eventually we were toiling forward unattended.

After a time even the gay decorations were discarded, we eagerly seeking the slightest opportunity of reducing every atom of weight possible, as, for every yard we stepped, our equipment appeared to increase its tonnage proportionately,

In addition to this galling burden we suffered great discomfort from the heat, and from the effect of the terrible cobble stones with which the road was paved. Although these stones appeared to the eye to be round and smooth, they attacked the feet with as much painful efficiency as red hot lances.

At mid-day a halt, very warmly welcomed by all, was called for refreshment, at least this was the term used by the officers, and with, I must admit, a large amount of justice as far as they were concerned. Marvels were executed with articles extracted from the dark depths of the officers' mess cart; within a few seconds a table covered by a snowy cloth, and groaning with the weight of tasty-looking viands, etc., to supply their needs, stood tantalisingly in sight of all. The field kitchens came along and discharged for *our* benefit, the outcome of their experiments with which we had to be satisfied, resigned in the knowledge that war was invented for the sole enjoyment of officers.

It was at this halt that I saw my first casualty of the war. The sight of us, apparently, had so upset or pleasantly excited, I am not certain which, although I strongly suspect the former reason, an elderly Frenchman that he collapsed and fell beside the road, and lay still, in a huddled heap.

Our first-aid men went to his assistance, but on examining him found him to be dead.

I must admit that we certainly were not looking as smart as possible when we projected ourselves on to his vision, but had no idea that we presented such an awful appearance as all that. In a large, open field that lay beside the road where we had halted, we discovered a turnip-like vegetable which we learnt was sugar beet. On tasting them I wondered why the persons responsible had seen fit to make use of the word 'sugar' in conjunction with this plant, as the only other flavour I could identify in addition to that of mud was one very similar to that possessed by strychnine. Compared, however, with the outrage the 'Black Squad' (cooks, save the name) had committed upon us, they were quite appetising, and I collected and consumed half a dozen of them in preference to the official meal.

After resting about an hour, we started off again, and very soon were made aware that the halt had not mended our sore feet. The cobble stones, indeed, appeared to make even more fiendish efforts to work their way through our boots.

After a while I became conscious of another pain, which, to a certain extent, succeeded in drawing my attention away from the trouble I was experiencing in my pedal extremities.

The symptoms of this fresh disaster were vaguely familiar, and were presently identified by a memory of my youthful past. I was forcibly reminded of a period of terrible anguish that had ensued hard upon an ill-advised raid on an orchard containing unripe apples. With this belated discovery of the cause of my distress, I had painfully acquired the knowledge that the only suitable place for sugar beets is in the ground.

The battle being waged in my lower regions slowly waned and allowed my attention to become engrossed by an anxiety concerning the whereabouts of my shoulders, which had apparently disappeared, and had been replaced by a couple of hefty bruises. On taking stock of my companions, I was selfishly pleased to find that they were suffering in a like manner.

Our equipment had, by this time, settled right down into each of us, with the weight and comfort of a five-ton lorry, while it was not necessary to mention our feet, for they protested for themselves; in fact, some of them attached to warriors who had neglected to

wash and powder them that morning created quite
a tumult.

I concentrated on presenting a bold front, attempting to console my injured feelings with the thought
that, after all, things in general had not been at all
bad, and this was the first hardship of any sort that
we had really experienced since leaving England. At
the moment, when our despondency had reached its
deepest depths, a pleasant little interlude occurred
which broke the weary monotony of our weary trudge,
and raised our drooping spirits considerably.

A silvery melody was dimly heard, a haunting, inspiring air, that neither increased nor diminished in
volume, although we were moving our position all the
time. This mystery intrigued us all mightily, until I
suddenly remembered the little clock that had been
presented to me by my French friends that morning,
before leaving Taisnieres. I drew it forth still bravely
performing, and displayed it to the admiring gaze of
my comrades, who subsequently demanded so many
encore performances that the works bade fair to drop
out with exhaustion.

In this way we continued our progress until, in the
early evening, we found ourselves passing an immense
fortification, swarming with French troops.

These troops of our Allies, the first we had encountered in the field, were vastly different in physique
and general appearance from the men that had met us
on the quay at Boulogne on our arrival. The defenders
of these forts were an extremely vigorous and healthy-
looking lot.

The forts appeared to be immensely efficient and powerful, were heavily armed with artillery of all calibres, and were surrounded by intricate earthworks and smothered with miles of barbed wire.

We, in our ignorance, judged them to be impregnable.

That our confidence in their strength was misplaced was to be proved within the next few days, for these were the famous forts of Maubeuge.

The garrisons of these strongholds rushed out and lined the route on our appearance, and shouted words of encouragement, to 'speed' us on our weary way, but speed had no particular attraction for any of us at that part of our pilgrimage; our boots were far, far too heavy.

'Esprit de corps', however, exerted its influence to such an extent that, at least while we remained in actual sight of our colleagues of France, we managed to stage a show that would have caused the Brigade of Guards to drop their 'arms' in sheer astonishment.

Maubeuge faded away in the dim distance behind us, and we sagged along with increasing exhaustion, until, with a happy sigh of intense relief, we received the command to halt on the outskirts of a village, where we were given instructions to prepare to spend the night, at which we all set to work with a will to make ourselves as comfortable as the circumstances permitted.

There were now unmistakable signs that the chances of contact with the enemy were not altogether remote.

Alarm posts were established, each company being allotted a position to which its members were to fly in

the event of an alarm being sounded during the night.
Upon these strategic positions the troops would be
able to rally without confusion.

Parties of men were paraded, and marched away to
perform outpost duty, a very businesslike-looking proceeding, which made war seem infinitely nearer, producing in us an air of eager expectancy, not unmixed,
as far as I was concerned, with a little trepidation.
Limits were set beyond which we were forbidden to
stray.

The institution of these restrictions was received by
us with a certain amount of cynical amusement.
Those of us who had fortunately escaped special duties
had taken advantage of the earliest opportunity to
remove our boots, and we lolled about all over the
camping ground, enjoying to the full the relief afforded
by this action. We had had quite enough roaming
for that day, and, in any case, thoughts of indulging
in such an unseemly pastime would have been immediately banished by the 'loud' protests emitted by
our weary feet. I devoted all my spare energy to the
task of providing a comfortable covering for the night.

The weather we had experienced up to that time had
been uniformly dry and hot, but on this particular
night there existed quite a mist or heavy dew, and I
considered it absolutely necessary to improvise some
means which would enable me to keep as warm and
dry as possible.

With this end in view, I consulted two men of my
section in the hope that by our combined efforts we
would succeed in producing the required shelter.

We reviewed the available materials. Each of us possessed, as a part of our equipment, a waterproof ground-sheet, about six feet by three. The borders being pierced with holes, reinforced by metal eyelets. Two of these sheets, laced together along one side placed over a pole about six feet in length, resting in its turn upon two sticks placed upright in the ground about two feet six inches high, make a very fine and cosy shelter, if the corners of the sheets are afterwards pegged securely down.

This method, although ideal, was out of the question, as we lacked the necessary woodwork.

We all walked about seeking anything in the shape of wood or any other article likely to answer our purpose, and, failing those, an inspiration; which eventually made its appearance.

After all, some people do use their heads for other purposes than to keep their hats off their shoulders.

The very thing to fulfil our requirements was discovered, in the shape of an empty and spacious G.S. wagon, a unit of our regimental transport. Had we been wise and experienced, its very convenience and emptiness would have aroused our suspicions, but to pass on, all that was required to transform that wagon into first-class sleeping quarters for three weary and deserving soldiers was the application of three waterproof sheets, laced soundly together, across the open top of the wagon, and lashed firmly down along the sides; then, when we were ready for bye-bye, all we had to do was to crawl in between the sheets and the floor of the wagon and drop off to sleep with as much comfort as it was possible to obtain under the circumstances.

This project was immediately put into execution, to our vast satisfaction and the undisguised envy of those who had grasped the possibilities of the wagon too late to be able to take advantage of them. Now that we had provided ourselves with a comfortable home, I took a look round the environs of our camping ground.

The field in which we were bivouacked lay immediately off a main road, and was separated from it by a ditch about five feet wide and three deep; this ditch was spanned at intervals by culverts, just about wide enough to permit the passage of ordinary farmcarts. On the other side of the road I espied an inn, upon which I immediately concluded my examination of the geography of our camp, and proceeded towards it in great haste.

I discovered that the best part of it had been commandeered to serve as an officers' mess, and the battalion headquarters, and, as usual, it had been placed out of bounds.

I found that quite a large crowd of troops had gathered in its vicinity, and stood in attitudes of the most profound dejection gazing with expressions of hopeless longing at several natives who were pleasantly engaged in enjoying the promising-looking contents of large glasses. We hung about this sight with as much purpose as a crowd of city clerks engaged in drooping over wooden barriers wasting their own and other people's time in gazing at a bunch of hard-working road-men-

ders ; only, in that case, the pleasure is derived solely
from watching other people perform the task, whereas
in ours, our chief desire was to do the essential part of
the job ourselves.

The action of our thirsty crowd inadvertently proved
to contain the elements of common sense, for after a
while, some of the jovial customers of the inn, being at
a loss to propound a satisfactory reason for our peculiar conduct in remaining outside the house of refreshment, deemed it essential, for their peace of mind, to
discover the cause.

Having appointed a deputation from among their
number, this body duly approached us to ascertain the
solution of our highly mysterious behaviour.

In no time, in spite of the language barrier, they,
being men of immense understanding, fully grasped
the position, and thereupon appointed themselves in-
termediaries between us and the proprietor of the bar,
by this means, happily, alleviating our acute suffering
and distress. By these means we were enabled to thwart
the unfeeling designs of those in authority.

Sparing a moment, during an interval occasioned by
the empty need of my glass, I glanced about, and saw
a large cart, drawn by an animal that I at first took
to be a dog on account of its lack of size, but which
subsequently proved to be a tiny ass, draw up outside
the inn.

The cart was loaded sky-high with greenstuff, which
commenced to heave about violently, each movement
causing the cart to tilt, and to lift the tiny steed clean
off its feet, until, eventually, from the midst of the

vegetables there emerged an elderly Frenchman, who tumbled out and sprawled in the roadway. Pulling himself together, he crawled into the 'pub'.

It was clear that inns had not been 'out of bounds' to him that day. Growls of pity for the poor little beast (I refer to the one between the shafts of the cart) arose from among our men.

Ninety per cent. of the regiment could lay claim to having seen their first dawn in the neighbourhood of the Bow Bells, and, consequently, most of them had been associated with donkeys (four-legged variety) all their lives.

The obviously unfair task set this mite aroused their ire, and many suggestions of ways and means to score off the owner were mooted. One, rather ancient, that I had previously seen pictorially presented, was received with the highest favour, and several resolute men proceeded to put it into execution.

Walking casually over to the donkey, they caught hold of its bridle, and led it gently out of the sight of anyone in the interior of the inn, to the side of the building, where there was a gate that gave admittance to a yard in rear of the premises. There they unharnessed the animal, wheeled the cart into the yard, closed the gate, and thrust the shafts out through the bars, and then replaced the donkey between the shafts, and harnessed to the cart with the gate dividing them.

The conclusion of this manœuvre presented the ridiculous and impossible spectacle of the ass, having apparently climbed through the four-inch space between the bars of the gate, and we greeted it with roars of merriment and approval, and the advent of the owner was awaited with considerable interest.

He took an exasperatingly long time to bring himself to the pitch of being susceptible to the urge of his home fire, but at last he stood, wobbling dizzily in the doorway, and we prepared to enjoy some great fun.

He staggered out into the roadway, looked about him uncertainly for a moment, and then, unconcernedly plunged away up the road towards the village, with the gait of a sailor traversing a deck in a heavy sea, and the air of an absent-minded professor. Chagrin overwhelmed us on discovering that our victim was apparently so intent on inward reflections that he had entirely forgotten the presence of his little friend, and so failed to provide us the entertainment we had arranged.

A decision to liberate the ass and to turn it loose had just been arrived at when the action was arrested by the sounds of staggering footsteps, growing momentarily louder. It was our friend returning. He had at last missed something, and had not been able to make up his mind as to the exact nature of his loss, for he stood in solemn thought on the spot on which he had originally left his possessions, until his wandering reflections were arrested by a large and loud bray which issued from the animal, an effort entirely out of all proportion to its size.

A vacant smile spread over the man's face, and he zig-zagged over and seized the reins, and casually attempted to walk off.

The outfit, naturally, didn't budge, and a great deal of tugging and, I fear, bad language, was indulged in, with no avail. That poor moke had as much chance of moving as the rock of Gibraltar.

I imagine that the donkey was just as much surprised at the unusual state of affairs as his master.

It slowly penetrated into the gap that existed between the Frenchman's ears that all was not as it should be, and he held an investigation.

The deductions he made from that must have been of a surprising nature, judging from the bewildered glances he alternately directed at the donkey and the small space it had evidently negotiated.

Overcome by amazement, he bowed his head upon his arms, and tried to work the thing out.

Finally, without a doubt, arriving at the conclusion that his steed had performed a miracle, he rushed wildly into the inn, whether to acquaint the other customers of its wonderful powers, or to toast the great feat, I was not able to ascertain, as, at this point, we were ordered to return to our camp.

Arriving at my improvised caravan, I found that my two partners had already gone to bed, and I made haste to do likewise, pulling on and closely buttoning up my greatcoat by way of preparation.

Inside, I told my bedfellows the story of the little tableau staged in front of the inn, and it was received with great laughter, and after a little further talk, of which the main burden consisted of expressions of pity for the poor devils of the battalion who had not displayed as much initiative as we had in securing such comfortable quarters, which was probably owing to to the fact, we complacently agreed, that they had been far from the front of the crowd when grey matter was being issued. We then subsided into peaceful slumber.

We were destined to have the happy air of peaceful bliss rudely torn from us.

I dreamt that night that as I lay asleep, looking as innocent as a little lamb, an eagle, soaring at a distance, a great distance, was so deceived by my remarkable resemblance to that harbinger of springtime, that he came to the conclusion that I was just the item necessary to satisfy his craving for food. Pouncing upon me with a shriek of joy, he bore me aloft in his talons. When he had reached an altitude of about a hundred miles, he took a good look at me, and, happening to sight my face, gave a wild thrill of horror, and released his hold on me in disgust.

Down, and still down, I spun and dived, until my further progress was arrested by the ground, which I struck with a terrific thump. As I slowly recovered consciousness, I found that my expectations had been realised, and that I had eventually arrived at the place I had so very often been consigned to during my sweet young life.   I was undoubtedly in a pit of some kind, and although I couldn't feel the effects of the fire I had been led to believe was the principal bogy of the place, I came to the conclusion that the lack of heat was due to the fact that the stokers were not as hard-worked as they were alleged to be. I was, however, soon made aware that other portions of the programme were to be

G

proceeded with, for the little chaps who perform, in expiation of their sins, the duty of prodding new recruits to their establishment with those nasty-looking toasting-forklike implements, seemed to be doing their job efficiently.

Gradually my faculties became concentrated on two of the blighters whose activities completely transcended the efforts of all the remainder combined.

One was viciously stabbing me in the left ear, while the other did his best to destroy my nose.

Their united efforts proved too much for me, and I really awoke with a wild shriek of rage and pain to discover that my two companions and myself were lying huddled up in the ditch separating the road from the field.

Our erstwhile home, the wagon, was lying canted precariously over us, with one of its rear wheels in the ditch.

With a sigh I removed the barrel of a rifle out of my left ear, and a heavy foot from the vicinity of my nose, and started up to ascertain the cause of our misfortune.

The explanation was remarkably simple.

The wagon we had honoured with our choice—above every other wagon in the whole British army—had to be the one detailed for a job in the middle of the night.

The driver had been instructed to proceed with it to a railhead to collect provisions.

Being very drowsy, and but half awake, he had failed to notice us and our little nest, and for the same reason he had also failed to negotiate the narrow culvert giving access to the road with the startling results we experienced.

We crawled brokenly away to the widest open space we could find and endeavoured to continue our rudely interrupted slumbers, feeling considerably chastened in spirit, recognising to the full the truth of the adage, 'There's nothing to be proud about after you have fallen.'

CHAPTER VIII

The following morning, the twenty-second of August, I awoke with the break of dawn, and found myself saturated with dew, and almost frozen by the chilly night air.

My condition rendered further thoughts of sleep out of the question, so I sprang up, and indulged, for about twenty minutes, in exercises calculated to restore my arrested circulation, and bring me to a reasonable state of warmth.

With the exception of the sentries and myself, the camp remained wrapped in slumber. I therefore decided to take a walk, and have a look at a village in our vicinity, which attracted my interest. On my way, I was suddenly startled by a loud whirring sound that started from almost under my feet, and a body, which I saw was that of a bird, hurtled up and away.

Overcoming my surprise, I directed my glances at the spot from which this unexpected apparition had materialised, to be instantly rewarded by a very fine sight which gladdened my heart. At my feet, very neatly and carefully arranged, lay a nest containing eleven eggs, the potential offspring of, I believe, a pheasant. I discreetly sampled one, and, finding it in excellent condition and quite fresh, quickly collected the remainder and placed them in my hat.

After carrying out my original intention of visiting
the village, I returned to the camp, and found that my
two companions of the unfortunate *contretemps* of the
preceding night were now awake. The sight, and a
promise of a share in my treasure trove, acted on them
as a *solatium*, and with the air of conspirators we stole
away to select a lone spot in which we could dispose
of them without interruption.

A little fire was soon blazing merrily, and we performed the necessary culinary offices, and thoroughly
enjoyed the succulent repast.

At this exhibition of my foraging abilities, my
companions passed a vote of confidence in me, which
restored to me my self-respect and the prestige I had
forfeited by the bad tactics I had displayed in the
selection of sleeping-accommodation of the preceding
evening. The meal over, we returned to the midst of
our company, where I was surprised by a visit from
dear old 'Pedler.'

He stood before me, and subjected me to a deep,
silent glance of reproach, the sight of which caused
my conscience to smite me sorely, for I suddenly remembered that I had neglected to seek him out the
night before, and correctly guessed that, as a consequence of my omission, he had not been able to
secure his usual pint or so of 'supper' before retiring
to bed.

I was really not guilty of any intention to ignore him
in this unfeeling manner, but on making my discovery
of the presence of the inn the previous evening I had
felt positive that 'Pedler' would be found among the

foremost in its vicinity. All my anxiety regarding him
had finally been banished from my thoughts by the
amusing episode of the donkey.

'Hullo! "Pedler," why so pale and ill-looking?' I
greeted him.

'Pale and ill-looking!' replied he sourly, 'I'm blinking
well dying of consumption; consumption of so-called
tea and filthy water. A hell of a pal you are! I sat all
the damned night in one spot, gambling upon you to
turn up and raise my "spirits ", afraid to move an inch,
lest it would result in you missing me. The only satisfaction I got from my misplaced trust in you is a fine
bunch of corns through sitting about so long. I finally
concluded that you had been sent away somewhere for
the night.'

I answered 'Pedler's' tirade by explaining 'but
for a little accidental intervention, his conclusion
would have been justified; and I told him of our
nocturnal adventure, the recital of which restored
him to his usual happy frame of mind, and, upon my
handing him half of my remaining cash to enable him
to bear any future separation with more reliance and
fortitude, he became quite amiable.

On completion of a meal that was now served, we
removed all evidences of our bivouacking attempts,
and tidied up the ground we had occupied, and
then paraded, to be subjected to a serious discourse
by our officers. We were warned that affairs had now
reached a stage that demanded the strictest attention
to discipline and all things appertaining to the preservation of the fighting efficiency of the regiment. It was

particularly impressed upon us, that, from that time onward, contact was likely to be established with the enemy at any moment, and in view of the gravity of future proceedings we were implored to cease treating the War as a picnic.

A pile of printed matter was then issued to us. One of them dealt with the explanations of French military commands and challenges. These were set out in three columns, the first column displaying the command or challenge in correct French. In the second the words were spelt phonetically, while the third column contained the English translation.

This leaflet, in particular, was very well received by us, and within a second of its receipt the whole camp resounded to the efforts of would-be French linguists, supplying a very fair imitation of Epsom on Derby day.

Fortunately for the majority of us, no occasion presented itself demanding the doubtful rendering of these exercises upon the soldiers of our Allies. Had a situation arisen, calling for an exchange of challenges and replies between the two nationalities, I have no doubt that the first French sentry to have his senses outraged and insulted by our barbarous mutilation of his beloved language, would have shot us out of hand, without the least hesitation. Another little pamphlet— quite a work of art this one—yielded to our admiring and curious gaze a number of neatly-coloured plates, portraying soldiers in the various uniforms worn by our Allies, and also those sported by the men of the German Army.

There was also a section devoted to the outlines and characteristics of various types of aircraft used by both the Allies and the enemy, illustrating their marks of identification.

This section received but scant attention as their use in warfare was not, at that time, appreciated or understood. We turned back, therefore, to the pages dealing with the enemy. These, rightly, claimed the greatest share of interest, and we scanned them with avidity. They became the subject of much discussion among us, which was only ended by the receipt of orders to parade in preparation to march.

The method of procedure now assumed a warlike aspect, and the column advanced in the manner prescribed by the eminent tacticians in authority, for troops operating in a hostile country.

When advancing in this formation the column proceeds, roughly, in the following order:

One lone soldier goes on ahead leading the way like a guiding star. He performs a duty known as 'point'.

He is followed by a chain of single files, each at an interval of fifty yards or more, according to the closeness or openness of the country through which the troops are moving.

The duty of these followers is to provide links to connect 'point' to the main body following in rear.

The whole idea underlying this form of progression is a desire to protect the main body against surprise, this sensation being reserved as the sole perquisite of the unfortunate 'Mr. Point'. To drive home to my readers the excellence of this plan, I propose to supply an illustration of the scheme actually in operation, based on an entirely suppositional march of this nature during the Great War.

'Point' was strolling along at the head of his army, more or less comfortably, according to his knowledge of the one particular reason for his being placed in such prominence, and to his powers of imagination.

He saw no signs of the enemy; but a portly 'Jerry', squatting out of his sight in a wood, swilling his morning soup, being compelled to come up for breath, spotted him.

With popping eyes, he excitedly rushed up to the under officer and gasped out: 'Mein Gott! Herr Under Officer, an enemy over there all midt himself is coming!' An orgy of mutual saluting, and the under officer dashed off to the nearest over officer, and, clicking his heels smartly, transferred his intelligence.

Herr Over Officer, with visions of a big Iron Cross looming in the offing, passed on the glad tidings with the utmost dispatch, and eventually, after passing through the usual channels, it reached the headquarters of the German High Command, where it was poured into the roomy ears of the Commander-in-Chief of the Imperial German Army.

Meanwhile poor 'Point' strolled happily along, oblivious of the excitement and interest he had created among his foes. The enemy Commander-in-Chief, on receipt of the astonishing tidings of 'Point's' unseemly conduct, roared in a great rage: 'Der Teufel Donnerwetter, and Damnationillstrafe', and rang up all the available artillery in his army and ordered them to

destroy the contemptible insect that had the temerity
to use the 'All-Highest's' road. 'Point', jogging blissfully along his way, suddenly disappeared for ever
from all human ken, and the connecting files justified
their existence by passing on the good news of his unexpected demise to the main body, thus securing them
against the unpleasantness of an experience of a similar
nature, and giving them ample cause to congratulate
themselves on their longsighted unselfishness in according 'Point' precedence. I have expounded the perilous
and arduous duties of 'Point' at great length, because
I feel that I owe it to myself to do so, for to me fell the
unsought honour of providing the battalion with a
'Jerry' alarm that day.

Setting out nervously, carrying myself with an air
of circumspection that would have done credit to a
burglar negotiating the obstacles in a china shop, full
of qualms and a feeling that I was cut off from the
world, and that I had every opportunity of finding
that morbid sensation *un fait accompli*.

Every building, or any spot capable of affording any
body cover from my view I approached with the utter-
most apprehension, my imagination liberally popula-
ting it with hordes of the Kaiser's Army.

Perspiration drenched me, and hundreds of times
during that journey I sensed the impact of the bullet
that would ring the 'alarm', as it were, upon my head.
A very unpleasant experience ; however, 'familiarity
breeds contempt,' and after a couple of hours I was
considerably thankful to note that the tension had
somewhat relaxed.

I had just settled comfortably to my job when I received my first real fright, for, on rounding a bend in the road, I suddenly caught sight of a mass of moving people and vehicles travelling on the road towards me.

I flashed back a signal to the column to halt, and leaped like a hare into a handy ditch, where I anxiously waited their nearer approach. When they had closed in upon my position I found that they were a motley crowd of civilians, composed mostly of women and children wearing dejected and hopeless expressions of resigned abandon, accompanied by carts, etc., piled with household utensils and furniture of every description, while all kinds of domestic animals were attached or driven in the rear.

An officer with a supporting party came up to ascertain the reason for the stoppage. He spoke at length with these people, who, he informed me, were refugees fleeing from the enemy. Although I had heard stories of people being driven from their homes by the advance of the German hosts, these were the first sufferers I had actually encountered, and they consequently occasioned me a great deal of interest, the more, when I learned that they had actually seen the enemy on the morning of the previous day. This intelligence, naturally, did not cause me to feel more amorous towards my ticklish job.

The thought of having us as a barrier between them and the enemy served to slightly raise the spirits of these poor unfortunates. I experienced great trouble with my swallowing apparatus as I watched them standing there so forlornly, weeping bitterly with grief and despair at the loss of their homes and almost the whole of their material earthly possessions.

This, to my mind, constituted the saddest spectacle of the whole War. Having recovered from the scare the appearance these pilgrims had occasioned me, I reluctantly continued my sacrificial progress. Feeling very sad for the refugees, and also for myself.

Many more of these homeless outcasts were passed at frequent intervals, as I continued on my way.

At about 3 p.m. I found that I had arrived on the outskirts of a very large town, and, in accordance with previous instructions given me for my guidance in such an eventuality, I halted, and passed the intelligence to the rear.

Officers, and a part of the battalion joined me, and after references to maps a party was dispatched into the town to reconnoitre. For the first time since the march had started, I really experienced the comfort of normal breathing, and I rested very much at my ease, happy for the moment with the consciousness of a task well done and the satisfaction of having, at any rate for the time, escaped becoming the main theme of an obituary notice. I resolutely dismissed all thoughts of the future, being a firm believer in the soundness of the maxim, 'Sufficient unto the day,' etc. The reconnoitring patrol returned and reported that the town was free of the enemy, and that it was safe to enter without fear of molestation, and we accordingly continued our interrupted advance, and for the first time in the history of the Great War British troops entered Mons.

On our arrival in the market square in this now famous town, we halted, and were supplied with a meal, while our commanders engaged in a very earnest conference.

I was extremely surprised after having met so many bands of refugees southward of Mons, fleeing from the results of battle and strife, to note that here the aspect was quite normal.

The market and the shops were doing brisk business, and the inhabitants moved about with a cheerful and apparently unconcerned air. The trams and the 'buses were being operated with vigour, and, on the whole, appearances were calculated to inspire the greatest confidence.

Our presence attracted the usual attention and curiosity, and the people crowded around us and treated us very kindly, giving us, without stint, all kinds of food and liquid refreshment, and above all, some much-desired cigarettes.

These good people of Mons were, unconsciously, experiencing the last moments of peace and happiness they were destined to enjoy for four long years, for a sad fate was to overtake them ere another twenty-four hours had barely elapsed.

Of this both we and they were happily in ignorance, and our advent among them was the subject of mutual congratulations. The officers rejoined us, and the word was passed round to prepare to advance once again.

Excitement soared to fever pitch on being informed by our company commander that the enemy was within striking distance of us. I hardly can tell whether this information made me feel glad or the reverse, but I do know, at least, I nursed a sneaking hope that as soon as the news of our arrival in the vicinity reached the ears of the enemy he would obligingly retire, and so enable the War to proceed under the fairly safe conditions that we had, until then, enjoyed.

The company of which I was an insignificant member was the first to leave the market square, and we moved off from the rest of the battalion, quite unconscious of the melancholy fact that this constituted the last view we would ever have of the majority of its members, and passed out to beyond the north of Mons.

When we had progressed about a mile from the outskirts of the town, we received our first big thrill of Active Service. We met a cavalry patrol, consisting of a squadron of our Dragoons, jogging along in the highest of spirits, bearing unmistakable signs of a victorious brush with the enemy, in the form of six captive Uhlans. On regarding this sight, our eyes bulged with excitement, and the superior air assumed by these 'veterans' of conquest and war roused our envy, but nevertheless we accorded them a hearty ovation, which they deigned to acknowledge condescendingly with smiles of great haughtiness and aloofness.

We pressed forward, filled with a mighty desire to emulate our cavalry colleagues in their doughty deeds of prowess, until we came to a wood, about three miles from our starting point, where we halted and took cover.

A party of us were detailed to go to a small hamlet consisting of half a dozen houses a few yards behind the wood, and to commandeer carts, ploughs, or any article likely to be of use in the construction of a barricade.

This was carried out with such zeal that within a few minutes, with the eager assistance of the natives, a powerful and efficient-looking barrier stood denying the passage of the road.

The result of our labours having been inspected and approved of by my company officer, he allotted to me and my section duties of a nature similar to those that at an earlier period in history were so ably performed by the brave Horatius, of Roman fame. The remainder of the company withdrew to the shelter and moral comfort of the wood, leaving me and my little party to guard our trust.

Double sentries were posted, with instructions to be particularly alert for signs of raiding bands of Uhlans, and, in general, we took ourselves very seriously, and awaited the outcome of events with a martyred air of a noble determination to do or to die.

The serious aspect with which he had invested the War was now marred by the appearance of crowds of curious women, girls, and children, who had rallied from the surrounding villages to view the strange sight we presented.

It became utterly impossible to retain the grave and noble air we had assumed for the occasion; how could we? when the greater part of our formidable-looking barricade was being utilised as a grandstand from which to observe the proceedings by a crowd of saucy wenches and children, while all the while they bombarded us with a single word that appeared to be the extent of their vocabulary, an iterated 'Souvenir?' 'Souvenir?'

This they coyly lisped while they fingered our remaining badges and buttons lovingly.

We hadn't the heart to resist these insinuating appeals, especially after an excellent medium of barter had been arranged, by mutual consent. Only the opportune arrival of orders to us to leave the barricade and rejoin the company enabled me to get away with sufficient buttons remaining to ensure the preservation of the common decencies demanded by civilisation.

A very determined lot of specimens of the species, these.

As soon as I had reported to my company, a move was made to take possession of a position about another mile ahead of us. While we were travelling to this new objective, a low humming sound was heard, the source of which was eventually traced to an aeroplane, the first we had seen in this War, flying in our direction at a height of about a thousand feet. A concerted and hasty reference to our pamphlets was made, and the newcomer was identified as a German 'Taube' machine of graceful design.

It passed directly over us, and when it was immediately above us we directed a brisk fire towards it, which apparently went near enough to occasion the pilot some alarm, for he at once set his course for the opposite direction, and melted away with all the speed at his disposal.

H

We were considerably crestfallen and disappointed at our failure to 'bag him', as we should easily have done, he being well within effective rifle range. I am afraid that this failure to accomplish our grim purpose was due to a lack of reasoning and forethought, occasioned by the great excitement his unexpected appearance wrought in us. On holding an inquest between us, we found that we had all aimed directly at the machine, without making any allowance for the speed of its flight, consequently our bullets passed harmlessly behind it. We passed a resolution to profit by this lesson in future.

Continuing after this disgusting exhibition of markmanship, we entered the grounds of a convent, the vicinity of which had been selected as a position for the establishment of a suitable outpost. This convent proved to be a school for young girls, and the Nuns and a large number of their pupils, who were between the ages of fourteen and eighteen years of age, half their number being, we were pleasantly surprised to find, British, gave us a tremendous welcome. They made us feel absolutely at home, when they, with charming kindness, supplied us with real English afternoon tea, including deliciously buttered bread, jam, and cakes.

The incongruity of the situation was amazing. Here we sat, on the brink of momentary precipitation into grim and bloody strife, amid peace and extremely pleasant surroundings, enjoying a jolly tea in the company of dainty little schoolgirls who, apparently, had no idea of the seriousness of the situation at that moment. They admitted that they had heard that the Germans were not far away, and confessed that they had, at one time, felt a wee bit scared, but now that we had arrived they felt quite safe and happy.

I always feel humiliated when I remember those expressions of their confidence and simple faith in our infallibility, and the knowledge that most of them were not present at the convent when we were blasted from our position fills me with gratitude. On this day, our battalion was engaged on out-post duty for the remainder of the Brigade, which lay in rear in the neighbourhood of Mons. It was, therefore, our job, in the event of making contact with the enemy, to delay him long enough to enable our main body to prepare to receive him.

We were aware, therefore, that there would be no question of seriously defending the position at the convent.

Our Company Commander interviewed the Mother Superior of the convent and explained the situation to her, and earnestly requested her to retire with her charges to safer quarters. This advice she promised to follow as far as the pupils were concerned, but for herself and her Nuns she entertained other ideas. She assured him that she had no fear of suffering injury in the event of an attack as she had provided ample protection.

She later led the way to some huge and powerfully constructed cellars beneath the convent, which were found to have already been furnished with articles of furniture that gave them the appearance of hospital wards, ready to cope with any need likely to arise, and she signified that these were entirely at our disposal should the unfortunate necessity present itself.

Within a few hours, many a badly torn man had occasion to bless the kindly forethought and courage of that noble woman.

A call to present myself to my Company Commander broke in upon my meditations, and I ascertained from him that I was to continue to act the rôle of the company's little guardian angel. How I craved for less popularity.

I was instructed to select six men of my section and to proceed and take up a position at a small cottage that could be observed standing by the side of the road running past our present position, about one hundred yards ahead. Here I was expected to pass away the night in anxious vigil, to ensure protection against surprise to my comrades in rear, and thus enable them to enjoy a sound sleep, which, of course, was not needed by me, free from care and worry, secure in the knowledge that the very best men to be found in the whole British Army were on the job (we kidded ourselves in this way by way of consolation) to stave off any inconsiderate attempt by the enemy to molest them.

We reconnoitred the terrain we were to guard.

The cottage, a small, single-storied building, standing about ten yards from the road, was locked and barricaded.

Upon breaking it open, we found that it was devoid of any article of furniture, and it had every appearance of having been abandoned some time.

Surrounding the building was an orchard, and in the direction of our front and rear this orchard was enclosed by a stout hedge.

On the right flank it was bounded by a wire fence and a small wood.

Along our left ran a road which branched off from a road crossing the front of our main position in rear, and continued until it was lost to our view where it curved and disappeared into a wood that stretched across the country along our front and away down our right flank.

This survey gave me poor satisfaction, and I formed the opinion that the situation was decidedly unfavourable, the particularly disturbing features being the immense wood on our front and the small wood on the immediate right.

I found that it was impossible to conjure up any appreciation of its decorative value to the landscape, for my mind was fully occupied by its tendency to leave a little too much to the imagination.

After careful consideration, I decided to form two posts, allotting two men to each one, for mutual and moral support.

For the position of the first I selected a point about fifty yards in front of the hedge bounding the orchard on our front; this commanded a clear view of the road up to the point where it lost itself from our sight behind the wood.

The second I placed about one hundred yards to the right, and in line with the first.

The other two men and myself I formed into a patrol.

We spent the whole night in a constant round of visits to the two posts, and in fearfully exploring the woods on our front and right. The performance of the latter part of this duty was heartily disliked by us all, and we passed the time occupied in the examination of these dark, forbidding places, with our hearts trying desperately to displace our tonsils, thrilled unpleasantly by the expectation of suddenly encountering something frightful.

I realised fully, during that night, how very fearless I wasn't. At the sight of the lighter effects appearing in the sky, betokening the lifting of the veil of darkness that enveloped us, I could have shouted aloud with joy.

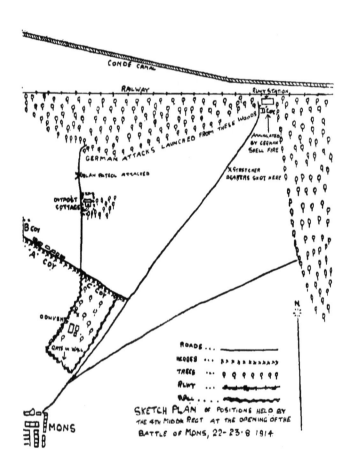

CONDÉ CANAL

RAILWAY   RLWY STATION

                                                        LOCK

GERMAN ATTACKS LAUNCHED FROM THESE WOODS

                                                    ANNIHILATED
                                                    BY GERMAN
                                                    SHELL FIRE

X ULAN PATROL ATTACKED

                                        X STRETCHER
                                        BEARERS SHOT HERE

OUTPOST
COTTAGE

B COY

A COY

C COY

CONVENT

GAPS IN WALL

N

ROADS . . . _____

HEDGES . . . ⋗⋗⋗⋗⋗⋗⋗⋗⋗

TREES . . . ♀ ♀ ♀ ♀ ♀ ♀ ♀

RLWY . . . ┿┿┿┿┿┿

WALL . . . .

SKETCH PLAN OF POSITIONS HELD BY
THE 4TH MIDDX REGT AT THE OPENING OF THE
BATTLE OF MONS, 22-23·8·1914

MONS

CHAPTER IX

A GLORIOUS dawn broke over the town of Mons and its environs on that Sunday morning of the twenty-third of August, 1914, heralding one of the most historical days in the annals of the British army, the remembrance of which will always be kept alive as long as the British Empire exists.

As for me and my little force, never had the sun been greeted by anyone more enthusiastically, for, although nothing of an untoward nature had occurred during the watches of the night, the tension had sorely exercised our untried nerves. Immediately I considered that the light was strong enough to warrant the move, I withdrew my advanced posts, and, with sighs of thankfulness, retired into the grounds surrounding the cottage. I deemed that one sentry was now all that was necessary to maintain a satisfactory watch on our front, and I posted him in a position on the near side of the hedge on our front, where he could command a comprehensive view of the road and the wood in front and would be able to immediately detect any suspicious movement without himself being visible to anyone approaching the post from his front.

I next took advantage of the daylight that was now flooding the country to improve my knowledge of my surroundings.

To my horror I found that between my right flank and a large forest in the distance there was a huge open space bearing no visible signs of life, which gave me the unpleasant impression that this flank was 'in the air' and entirely unprotected, and that it had been in this condition all through the preceding night, a very serious matter, of which I fortunately, for my peace of mind, had remained in ignorance.

Suddenly, however, my roving eyes were attracted towards a large building lying in the woods on my right front, which I later ascertained was a railway station.

In and around this building there were lively signs of the presence of a large body of troops.

After close observation, I satisfied myself that the occupants were British, to my great relief, a conclusion I arrived at by watching a section of men coming from the direction of our rear, proceeding towards it, until I eventually saw them enter. The discovery that our troops were holding this 'strong point', about four hundred yards on my right flank, afforded me lively additional feelings of security.

Having thus oriented myself anew with the situation, we all retired, with the exception of the sentry, into the cottage, where I busied myself in preparing a report on the events, or lack of events, of the preceding night, for the benefit of my company officer. During the time I was occupied in this manner I observed one of my command conducting a weird and unsavoury experiment.

We were all gasping with a desire for a smoke, and were without the means of satisfying it.

Finding himself unable to control his longing for this soothing medium, this 'hero' produced from his pocket an almost exhausted packet of cigarette papers, and turned out his pockets in an unavailing search for tobacco. Disappointed, he hunted around for a substitute for the usual fillings.

His choice finally fell on the only thing available, the dried droppings of a horse, which he carefully collected from the road. He gravely pounded this mess between his palms in the approved manner, until it was reduced to a condition that met with his approval. He then rolled it up in a cigarette paper, and proceeded to smoke and inhale the result with the greatest sang-froid.

His expressions of complete enjoyment and satisfaction were so beguiling that I was almost persuaded to try the unusual mixture myself, but my stomach was not strong enough to permit me to make the attempt.

One of the men, prowling about the vicinity of the cottage, had discovered and unearthed the cover to a well. Taking advantage of this, we lowered our canteen, by means of our putties into it, and drew up some water, in which we enjoyed a very refreshing and much needed wash.

These ablutions having been completed, we were resting comfortably against the wall on the sunny side of the building when our sentry suddenly made an unheralded appearance before us.

His untoward proceeding in deserting his post astonished me considerably, and I was about to act the part of a hard-boiled sergeant-major of the old school to him when my flow of choice expletives, specially manufactured for the occasion, was arrested by the peculiar expression of suppression visible on his countenance, and his frantic efforts to overcome and control some frightful emotion sufficiently enough to enable him to get rid of something that was almost causing him to burst.

His heroic efforts were suddenly rewarded, and gave vent in a startled: 'Blimey! Corporal, grab your bloomin' pop-gun and come and have a "dekko" at the Kaiser's bodyguard prancing down the road, but be bleedin' careful.'

Wondering what on earth he was talking about, I decided to investigate, and, advancing by the methods employed by all the very best Red Indians when on the war-path, we crawled carefully to the post of observation.

What an unexpected eyeful greeted us. Coming carelessly along the road towards us was a Uhlan patrol consisting of seven or eight men, then a scanty eighty yards away.

The surprising nature of the sight robbed us of our breath and wits, and left us standing in a row gasping and looking like a lot of cod-fish.

The scene impressed me so strongly that it will always remain vividly engraved on my memory.

This was, actually, our first encounter with the enemy under arms, which may, to a certain extent, excuse the paralysis into which we were thrown. This suspended state of affairs was swiftly converted into deadly action when the man evidently in command of the enemy party suddenly gave vent to a stentorian roar and opened fire upon us with a pistol he had conjured from somewhere about his person. For an instant, unable to resist the overpowering impulse to seek protection from this spiteful outburst, we all bobbed down as though the ground had suddenly opened from beneath us, but in less than a split second, conquering our feelings, we pulled ourselves together and bobbed up again, filled with resentment at the unsportsmanlike conduct displayed by our opponent, just as the remainder of that misguided patrol had finally made up their minds to render their superior officer active support.

A short and vicious burst of rapid fire from us completely annihilated that little group with an ease that was staggering. In a second, the only living survivors were five poor chargers, that, rendered riderless, and being unharmed, turned and galloped back with snorts of terror towards the direction from whence they had appeared, until they gained the sanctuary of the wood, and disappeared from our view.

Immediately the excitement abated, and we stood aghast, overcome with horror by the enormity of the thing we had done.

We had dispatched fine, big, healthy men, full of the joy and the vigour of the prime of life, into the great unknown with scarcely a warning. We were all, I believe, absolutely stunned by the shock of this revelation, and at the ease with which it had been accomplished. We stood trembling like a forest of aspen trees for some time, amid an unbroken and deathly silence. I felt, unaccountably, physically sick. I was possessed of a guilty feeling of the kind that, I should imagine, floods the breast of a person who stands gazing down at the body of a victim of his murderous assault.

I had a distinct fear of the consequences of breaking one of the most solemn laws of civilisation.

I remained in this unpleasant state for quite a while, then, moistening my dry lips, and succeeding, after a stupendous effort, in recovering my usual self to some extent, I proposed that a man accompany me, and crawl out and examine the motionless figures to discover if any of them remained alive, and if so to bring them in as prisoners. Accompanied by a volunteer, we approached the frightful scene slowly, and with great circumspection. On arrival, we found that, without any doubt, they had all been killed, the majority of them bearing at least two marks as evidence of the terrible accuracy of our fire. Neglecting precaution, we stood looking down at the sad fruits of our first clash with the enemy, the sight of these dead men exercising a dreadful fascination for me which I found very difficult to dispel. Thrusting aside its baneful influence, I pulled myself together with an effort, and we collected the peculiar head-dress of these unlucky men. We returned with them to the cottage, arriving there without molestation on the part of the enemy, in which we were exceedingly fortunate, as I learned by later experiences that increased my knowledge of warfare; for it was by the one chance in hundreds that these Uhlans had not been followed closely by others, who would have made us pay for our curiosity, probably with our lives. In the safety of the precincts of the cottage we exhibited the trophies of War, which were carefully examined, amid the expressions of pride and admiration.

I dispatched a man to the company officer with a comprehensive report, acquainting him with the details of the skirmish, and also the helmets taken during the engagement as proof of our efficiency and prowess.

When the messenger returned, he bore a very welcome can of hot tea and some food of sorts, and was accompanied by a sergeant, who I thought, with relief, had appeared to take over the responsibilities of my command, but his only object was to survey the situation, on the completion of which he was to return and report it to the company commander.

On the termination of his investigations, the sergeant became frivolous and handed me instructions to hang on to my position, and to refrain from retiring on any account, until the receipt of definite orders to do so, and I was also to report without fail any further development of activity on the part of the enemy, or any signs of him, without loss of time.

Concluding this very excellent advice, he left to return to the rear with the air of an adventurer, his departure being viewed, on my part, with a certain amount of sorrow and regret.

I now issued orders to the men to select positions of vantage from which they could obtain the best view with the minimum amount of exposure, and to station themselves at them, and keep a close watch in the direction from which the enemy had appeared. Exercising, as I thought, very clever strategy, I mounted upon a cupboard fixed to the wall in the interior of the cottage, the top of which was within five feet of the sloping roof. From this I removed several small tiles, thus forming an orifice, about one foot square, through which I was able to obtain a splendid outlook over the ground in front, without, as I fondly imagined, being myself visible to anyone coming from the direction of the enemy.

One of the men got up beside me, and we constituted the position our watch-tower.

An astonishingly peaceful air pervaded the country-side, only belied by the awful spectacle on the road.

Church bells chimed sweetly in the towns and hamlets about us, and dimly, from the distance, we discerned faint strains of music being poured out at the service being held in the convent in our rear.

A lark hovering immediately above our hole in the roof trilled out a glorious burst of song, and we craned our necks the better to view it.

A strange and undefinable sense of unreality stole over me, and, for some extraordinary reason, I became attacked by a strong desire to cry. I endeavoured to impart my sensations to my colleague, and I said to him: 'There is something so extraordinary hanging about in the air, that I feel that the thing I would most enjoy would be a visit to a church. I don't like this quietness and——'

'SMACK!' the tile within two inches of our heads was shattered into a thousand fragments, and, incontinently, the two of us flopped simultaneously to the floor far beneath us.

I arose with an effort and continued in a quavering voice: 'I was about to add that I harboured a feeling that something startling was bound to happen to break the spell!

We did not need telling that the violent blow sustained by the tile above us was the result of a direct hit by a well-directed bullet.

Grinning sheepishly, we gathered ourselves together, feeling bruised and sore, and considerably alarmed, and each of us tenderly passed a hand over his anatomy to ascertain if any more serious damage had been done. Congratulating one another on our narrow escape, we concluded that a nice black hole, filled with a couple of moonlike faces, presented too good a target to be missed twice in succession, and we carefully selected another point from which to conduct our observations.

We had scarcely occupied our new post, when, on the centre of the road, at the point where it first became visible to us at our side of the wood in front, appeared a gigantic German infantryman. He stepped mincingly, and obviously unwillingly, towards our ambush, accompanying each pace with glances of the deepest apprehension in every direction.

I

I held my hand, being overcome by a kind of fellow-feeling and sympathy for him, for it was painfully clear to me that the poor beggar was performing the duties of my old friend 'Point.' Unmolested, he approached to within a bare hundred yards of us, when a section of about a dozen men appeared following in his wake. It was his 'Wake.'

A shot snapped out upon the peaceful air, fired by one of my men who could not control himself any longer, and poor old 'Point,' having justified his existence, passed out of the picture for ever. His comrades seeing him fall, halted uncertainly, no doubt shocked into immobility by alarm and rendered unable to make a decision regarding their proper procedure under these circumstances. We helped them out of this little dilemma with a well-directed shower of hot fire, upon receipt of which those that were still physically capable dashed madly back into the wood, leaving a pathetic group of still bundles as a tribute to our marksmanship.

I had time, after this outburst, to realise with something of a shock, that, strangely enough, the feeling of horror that I had experienced after the casualties we had inflicted upon the Uhlan patrol had now entirely disappeared, and had even been superseded by a wild and eager desire to kill and maim as many of the enemy as possible. We had, in fact, become transformed into killers. Like the killers of every species, it only required the first taste of blood to wash away all restraining barriers that ages of civilisation had painstakingly erected around us.

I have never failed to be amazed at this awful re-action, which deals a man an incalculable moral injury.

We now experienced our first real baptism of fire, as from the wood in front a steady fire was opened upon us, gradually increasing in its volume.

At first this caused us to be affected by strong desire to emulate the ostrich and to bury our heads into the ground, and to fire our rifles without taking any aim—a mistaken idea apparently underlying the action, that the more noise made the less chance there was of being harmed. This unsoldierlike conduct was eventually overcome, and after a short time we efficiently en-gaged in returning a smart, and, as we fondly hoped, effective reply.

My sensations during this baptism were too numer-ous and confused to analyse. I clearly remember being reduced to a profuse state of perspiration, the sweat pouring down my face and into my eyes in such volume as to render me temporarily blind. Gradually I became cooler, and the only sensation then noticeable was one of grim and increasing interest in this business of slaughter. Gone were all thoughts of fear, of danger and of mercy. Having become quite cool, and once more efficient, my thoughts cleared, and I was able to recollect that part of my orders demanding instant attention to the dispatch of a report on this new development in the situation to my company com-mander. I dashed off a note and handed it to the man on my immediate right, giving him instructions to get to the rear with it with the greatest dispatch.

He sprang up to carry out this project, and immediately collapsed with a bullet through his shoulder. Almost at the same time, another man was shot through the head.

I hurriedly selected another messenger, and sent him upon the same errand, and he returned, crawling, within half a minute, shot through both legs.

A small body of the enemy at this juncture made a tentative sortie from the right of the wood, but although our numbers were sadly depleted, we gave a display that persuaded them not to be so foolish. The position was now assuming awkward proportions, and I was about to try to get another messenger through when we were all considerably relieved to find that a welcome reinforcement had appeared, consisting of an officer and a platoon, who had been attracted by our heavy musketry fire, and had come up to discover the cause, which rendered a timely intervention on our behalf.

The officer now assumed command, and distributed his forces in the most advantageous manner, the advice given by us 'old and experienced' campaigners receiving flattering attention; and upon the newcomers catching sight of our victims, we were regarded with a certain amount of respect, not unmixed with awe. The enemy again resumed his attempts to feel out our strength by sending out small sections from the wood.

They were met by a withering fire each time that blew them back to their starting-point, with an impression, I should imagine, that we were several millions strong.

The officer eventually decided to evacuate this position and to retire on to the company. The wounded were first collected and sent to the rear, and when they were safely clear we followed, the officer warning us to leave as quietly and carefully as possible to avoid advertising the fact of our retirement to the enemy. He must have mistaken us for film stars. The only thing remotely resembling publicity desired by me at that time was expressed fully in the first syllable.

Wriggling back like a convoy of earwigs, we arrived at the position held by the main body without further casualties, and I proudly made my way to the presence of the company commander to render a report of the various actions in which I had been engaged that morning. He heard me through without a tremor, not evincing the slightest signs of emotion or admiration that I fully expected, and on the conclusion he dismissed me with a cool and curt nod. I thought over this casual treatment, and came to the conclusion that the news of the crushing defeats I had inflicted upon the enemy had conveyed to him the unpleasant conviction that the enemy would now probably be so dispirited and scared that he would rush back headlong to the Fatherland without giving our good captain a chance of enjoying the War at all. To put it in a nutshell, his cool treatment of me was prompted solely by motives of professional jealousy [*sic*].

To describe the position held by 'C' Company, of which I was a member :

A road traversed its front which was bordered on one side by a thick hedge that enclosed the grounds of the convent on its northern side.

The company commander had taken advantage of this natural obstacle to the enemy's advance by entrenching the company behind it.

A high stone wall, extending from our flanks to and along our rear, formed the other three boundaries of the convent grounds.

'A' company of the battalion held some houses in a small hamlet on our left, with their left flank protected in turn by 'B' Company.

'D' Company occupied the railway station, referred to by me previously in this chapter, and its environs, this position being about five hundred yards away on our right front.

At about one hundred yards from the front of the company's main position, directly ahead, was the little cottage that had been the scene of my outpost's first conflicts.

My little force became the centre of an admiring crowd of 'untried' soldiers, who bombarded us with innumerable questions of our impressions of being under fire and our idea of the German as a soldier. To this latter query we replied very disdainfully, the results of our engagements with him that morning showing him to be, in our 'experienced' opinion, nothing but a big bluff.

Our airy discourse was somewhat hurriedly curtailed by the sound of a fusillade of shots, not far enough away to be comfortably ignored.

Investigation showed that they were emanating from the cottage that had been my old outpost, and from the wood flanking it. The enemy had at last found that we had left it in his favour, and he was now making preparations with a view to inducing us to retire still farther.

We took up position to return his fire, which had not the least effect on my nervous system, I was pleased to note, and left me feeling quite cool and blasé. Curiously I devoted myself to a study of the others who were in sight, very much in the same spirit in which the old boys at school regard newcomers.

The comparison of their demeanour with that of my comrades of the actions of the morning furnished food for reflection.

The 'veterans' were about the only ones really doing any useful shooting, as they lay coolly and deliberately taking careful aim and firing. Most of the others were seemingly engaged in trying to work their passage to Australia via the shortest route, in fine, behaving exactly as we had done during the initial stage of our own baptism of fire. In the same manner, they, too, soon improved in their bearing, and before long were taking a decided interest in the War.

A lull in the musketry battle occurred, the enemy ceasing his fire, a move we at once seconded.

Shortly afterwards a solid phalanx, composed of several hundred 'Boche', advanced upon our defence in massed formation, from the wood. (I never could conjure up any passion for that wood.) Their solid, smart, military appearance as they strode heavily towards us, made an awe-inspiring spectacle.

An order was rapidly passed along the line warning every man to hold his fire until the company commander himself gave the order to open up.

We lay in a deathly and uneasy silence, all our faculties being concentrated on controlling the fearful desire to fire into that steadily advancing horde, who appeared to our tense imagination to be about to step upon us and overwhelm us with their numbers and weight.

All grimly hung on awaiting, with eager expectation, for the long delayed order that would relieve the enormous tension.

'What the hell is wrong with the captain; does he expect us to bite 'em?' queriously inquired a voice.

With the enemy not more than fifty yards away, it came:

'Rapid fire!'

That solid-looking field-grey wall was blasted away by the hail that leapt at them through the hedge, as powerful rifles, manipulated by men who, in pre-war days, depended on their skill at this exercise for their pay, pumped steel-jacketed leaden death into them, with never a miss, at the rate of at least fifteen rounds a minute per man. No troops on earth could have faced that murderous blast and existed, and within less than a minute of the order to fire, the only signs left of this futile attack, and of the terrible lesson the enemy had been taught, were the numerous, grey-clad figures that littered the ground between our hedge and the wood from which the enemy had launched his attack.

Another calm period ensued, broken only by the pitiful cries of the wounded foe who had been left lying abandoned out upon the blood-soaked field. Neither side could venture to their relief for the present, any proposed effort being restrained by the thought that the action would probably be misunderstood and rewarded by death, and there they continued to lie, writhing in great agony, unattended and without succour or relief.

Eventually their cries and groans became so intolerable that it was decided to take a chance and to form a rescue party, for service with which several of the men volunteered without hesitation. Their good intentions were arrested just as they were about to be put into execution, by the appearance of another avalanche of the enemy soldiery.

We could not deny the fact that they were game. In our opinion their commanders must have been imbeciles to send them against us again, in view of the obvious futility of the proceeding, which was made so very patent by the pitiful indication of the results of the previous attempt, that strewed the path of their proposed advance.

We met the new attack, employing precisely the same tactics as before.

The enemy came forward, displaying a marked depreciation in the air of confidence that characterised his previous onslaught, the loss of which he endeavoured to replace with a loud and frequent shouts of 'Hoch', accompanied by bursts of fire from the units of the front rank, which did us no harm, as their rifles were manipulated from the hip as they advanced in a desperate attempt to encourage themselves in their task, and, no doubt, to instil us with frightfulness.

All to no purpose, for again they were completely shattered by our outburst and thrown back decimated and in utter confusion, the mute evidence of their failures to penetrate into our position leaving us appalled and sick with slaughter.

After this abortive attempt to gain their objective the enemy apparently arrived at last at the same conclusion that we were better left alone, and we enjoyed a period of complete tranquillity.

Parties of enemy stretcher-bearers made their appearance, greatly to our relief, and entirely without interference, were permitted to carry out their errands of mercy.

The enemy losses in these two attacks amounted to hundreds in killed and wounded, while the only casualties suffered by us were five men slightly wounded, we having fought their attacks, made in the open upon us, from well-concealed cover.

CHAPTER X

An air of calm and peace once more reigned over the scene, the only visible signs of war being supplied by the enemy stretcher-bearers working out in front at their gruesome tasks.

It was necessary for some of these, during the course of their employment, to come within thirty yards of the hedge behind which we were entrenched and they interested us tremendously, especially when one or two of them hailed us in our own language.

This resulted in a great deal of chaffing, which was given and received by all with great good humour.

One of our wags, very unfeelingly, with an immense lack of tact, implored them to inform him 'how they liked their eggs fried', which drew the extremely rueful reply that we were inclined to season them with a little too much pepper.

As they were retiring on the completion of their job, one German, with a great grin, shouted :

'Next time you will make the visits to us!'

'You're wrong there, cocky, I can't abear agoin' ter cemeteries,' cheerfully answered our wit.

The calm was next shattered by the sounds of loud explosions, which focussed our attention on the railway station upon our right. Large puffs of smoke, centred by brilliant flashes, filling the air all about it, taught us that it was claiming the interest of the enemy artillery.

One shell, bursting against the roof of this building and sending a shower of debris in all directions, signified that at last the correct range had been obtained.

Immediately the station became enveloped by the bursting of a storm of shells and a pall of smoke which converted its erstwhile peaceful atmosphere into a raging, vomiting volcano, hurling its streams of wreckage and amputated limbs and bodies high into the air, and within less than ten minutes it was completely demolished and its defenders annihilated.

This ghastly catastrophe affected us terribly and altered our previous comfortable feeling of superiority and safety. The destruction of this position gave us our first lesson of the overwhelming effect of artillery fire, and the ease and speed with which this well-built edifice had been reduced to dust instilled into us great and somewhat fearful respect for heavy-gun fire. This exhibition also implanted in us a feeling of anger and resentment against the enemy (we, quite unreasonably, entertaining an idea that using this unfair means to gain his ends he was behaving in an unsportsmanlike manner) so powerful, that we regretted the courtesy that we had extended owards his stretcher-bearers. The rage and hate we now bore him was further enhanced, and brought to a pitch of howling fury, by an exhibition of cowardly conduct on the part of some German riflemen.

A section of British, bearing stretchers, each one of them unarmed, proceeding from our rear, past our right flank towards the ruins of the railway station, on a perfectly obvious errand of mercy, were suddenly fired upon. Their leader and two others fell to the ground, apparently hit, and their comrades stopped and administered aid. A slight pause, and then they continued calmly upon their way towards their objective, supporting two of the victims of that murderous assault they had carefully assisted to rise from their prone positions into which they had been stricken, leaving one still form lying where it had fallen, to remain for ever beyond all human help. Although they were now aware that they were moving amid the enemy, and were fully exposed to them with every chance of receiving additional brutal evidence that the 'Boche' was no respecter of the Law of Nations, they gallantly went forward to the succour and comfort of their torn and bleeding comrades, without evincing the slightest sign of hesitation or fear of the consequences.

The leader, who had paid for the venture with his life, was the corporal who had induced me to exchange duties with him while we were staying in the town of Taisnieres.

Among the number of these heroes I was pitifully shocked to recognise my old chum 'Pedler', whom I have never again seen, to this day.

As these men continued towards their original objective, resolved at all costs to execute their noble errand of mercy, we watched their progress with bated breath and teeth clenched in an agony of dreadful anticipation. We momentarily expected the enemy to renew his unwarrantable attack upon the unfortunate stretcher bearers in spite of the fact that the nature of their duties must have been perfectly obvious to him.

Either amazement, or admiration at their cool daring, stayed the hands of the enemy from further ungallant outrage, for, without any further molestation, they slowly wended their selected way, until they were lost to the sight of our aching eyes.

I saw many a man weeping aloud, unashamedly, at the blackguardly and unchristian attack on that gallant band, and many were the curses and oaths to avenge the death of the unfortunate corporal that filled the air as we feverishly searched our front for any enemy target that would afford us an outlet for our outraged feelings. As though in answer to our blood-thirsty desires, a wonderful opportunity was presented to us, promising complete satisfaction, and bidding fair to sate our inordinate lust to exact reprisals.

We, filled with the feelings of fiercest joy, now beheld our particular section of the German army once more emerging from the point from which they had launched their previous abortive attacks.

Appearing as solid as a wall, they came towards us in perfect alignment, wearing looks of grim determination that bade ill for us should success attend their efforts. There existed a subtle difference in the bearing of these new attackers when compared with our former visitors, and they were also of bigger physique and of smarter appearance.

I could see some officers waving swords as they rushed 'bravely' to and fro, well behind the rear ranks of their men, exhorting them to press forward and collect the due that was coming to them. In my great confidence in our ability to deal satisfactorily with this menace I permitted myself to consider that this sortie was nothing but a rash urge to court suicide, and their craving for this end filled me with amazement.

They had carefully prepared a little surprise for us this journey, undoubtedly based on their observation of our manner of meeting their first two attacks, particularly our habit of reserving our fire until they were almost on the top of us, for when they had covered half the distance between us and the wood a shrill bugle call rang out, which stirred the whole mass, as one man, into a charge towards us.

The use of these tactics carried them so close to us that we almost singed the eyebrows from over their staring eyeballs, as we emptied the contents of our rifles into their very faces. With the exception that their dead were left lying nearer our hedge than had been the case before, and that their attack had lasted just a little longer, for the only reason that the numbers to be disposed of were greater, this latest attack had produced no different results than their former.

The troops employed against us in this attack were the famous, and alleged invincible, Prussian Guard. We obtained this information from the shoulder straps on the corpses lying piled upon the ground in front of us, so near that the titles were plainly visible and easily read.

This knowledge put us in high humour, but the terrible price we had exacted from the enemy in payment for the treachery of his colleagues did not obtain our forgiveness or soften our hearts towards him, a fact that we clearly impressed upon him when he brazenly sent out his stretcher-bearers again. Notice to them that their activities would not be permitted was conveyed by a volley directed, not actually at them, but close enough to induce them to hop back to cover and accept the hint to remain there.

The enemy, after this, apparently decided to remain concealed and to content himself by directing a desultory fire upon our position, being, at last, perfectly satisfied with the collection of harps for that morning.

We now remarked upon a fact that the enemy seemed to lack the very elements of musketry, judging by the results he was obtaining from the tons of lead he was endeavouring to throw over to us. Although the air was full of the whine of bullets, they were much too wide of their targets to cause anyone of us the slightest inconvenience, nor did they appear likely to, and the results of this protracted musketry attack displayed an appalling degree of inefficiency from his point of view, but which was quite all right as far as we were concerned. This bred in us an air of contempt that induced us to treat this feeble show of lack of marksmanship with so much disdain that we experts would not bemean ourselves to the extent of replying to it.

Over an hour had passed since the enemy's last visit to us, or of any sign of his intention to come again, and the consequent lack of warlike occupation was producing a spirit of boredom in us.

The monotony became so pronounced that we were ready to welcome anything that would tend to disperse it, for that is what we believed in our sublime ignorance; we were destined to receive enlightenment upon that debatable point within a very short space of time.

Somebody created a slight stir of bored amusement by shouting: 'Sergeant! please can I go over to the woods to catch one of those nice little sausage wallopers? I want something to play with!' This display of foolishness the sergeant treated with the contempt it deserved.

All signs of fear had by this time left us, and we looked across at the evidences of our handiwork with a callousness that a few hours previously we would have regarded in others with loathing and contempt.

We had discarded all thought of taking advantage of the little protection we had at our disposal in the shelter offered by our trench, deeming such occupation not worthy of war-tried 'veterans,' and so we lounged about all over the place, with the most unconcerned air imaginable.

A new and peculiar sound, slight at first, but growing each instant in volume, disturbed our comfortable meditations. The only thing we were sure of about it was that it was undoubtedly something coming to us from the direction of Prussia, and we idly wondered whatever on earth it could be.

With as much noise, and sounding suspiciously akin to 'The Flying Scotsman', something passed over our heads, and ended its mad career in a terrific explosion

L

against a tower attached to the convent in our rear. Our surmises as to the identity of this stranger were ousted by a complete knowledge, and the speed in which we emerged from our somnambulistic attitudes and vaulted into that trench, having overcome suddenly our former scruples regarding the unsoldierly conduct of such a proceeding, was so amazing that it would need to be seen to be believed.

Long before that shell had even concluded its burst, there was not an eyelash remaining outside the only shelter available. A breathless silence ensued, broken suddenly by a quavering voice, bleating: 'Don't let that put the wind up yer, mites, they're quite sife when yer 'ears 'em. An old "swaddy" told me as yer carn't 'ear the one coming wot 'its yer,' a statement that was greeted by hysterical and inane laughter.

The old soldier who had proferred this consoling advice must have been referring to the period that follows immediately *after* the shell has scored a hit, and to have acquired his information on the subject secondhand, much after the same manner that the cabinboy of repute was wont to receive mysterious tales from his captain. I am entitled to write with authority on this question, having had several opportunities in which to prove conclusively, to my own satisfaction, the unsoundness of this theory. It is decidedly erroneous. We speculated, on recovering slightly from the scare given us, on the effect that shell had produced upon the inmates of the convent, and sincerely hoped that they had escaped injury.

Our fears for their welfare were removed, to a certain

extent, by the report of an officer who had just returned from a visit to the Mother Superior. He stated that all the pupils and the majority of the nuns had left for Mons, and comparative safety, and the Mother Superior, with a few Nuns that remained, were safely ensconced in the depths of their cellars.

We now had all our thoughts concentrated on the sounds of the approach of more shells, of which the first was the herald. They came our way with increasing frequency, each succeeding one exploding nearer to us, until one of them, at last, burst clean into the trench, knocking out at least half a dozen of the defenders. With blanched faces, we awaited the holocaust, for the spectacle of the bombardment of the railway station vividly projected itself before us, and taught us exactly what we had to expect.

The heavens seemed to open up and to spout fire and iron, and hell broke out around us. Every inch of our trench appeared to be drunkenly surging and erupting amidst a staggering din, above which could be distinguished the horrible shrieks of dying and shattered and dismembered men.

To this fiery onslaught we could oppose no effective reply, as the men who were thus destroying us piecemeal were probably miles away, and beyond our reach. We couldn't do a thing except to wriggle and claw about in the earth, in an ecstasy of horror.

To add to our discomfiture, a strong body of the enemy, having worked his way around, appeared on our right flank and enfiladed us with a deadly hail of machine gun fire

I, strange, though it may seem, welcomed this diversion, and, with several others near me, engaged with the authors of this flank attack, an action which considerably distracted our minds from the frightful havoc being caused by the shells.

A fresh discovery that our ammunition supply was almost exhausted made our position seem hopeless, an outlook which became practically confirmed by a report that the enemy was also delivering an attack from our other flank.

We were by this time almost completely surrounded, and it looked very much to me that we would soon be engaged in our last desperate defence at the point of the bayonet.

A few minutes before, we had been praying for something to turn up to relieve us of the monotony enveloping us. It had turned up all right, with a vengeance. Well, we ought to have been satisfied now, but I can give my honest assurance that I wasn't.

At the crisis, the company commander, who had very gallantly, right through the whole of this action, set us a wonderful example of coolness and courage, and who, by a miracle, was still to be numbered among the survivors of this hell, decided on a very perilous move, which, however, could not possibly make our chances of extinction any more certain, and ordered us to retire.

With a shout of defiance, what was left of the company turned and rushed through the grounds of the convent.

Arriving on the far side, we found that further progress was barred to us by a wall about ten feet high, in which was set a stout iron gate, securely locked.

We were trapped, and stood helpless, targets for a blast of machine gun fire that rained mercilessly upon us, effectively reducing us to still smaller numbers. Grimly we fixed our bayonets, and prepared to end the unequal struggle and suspense in a mad charge into those murderous machine-guns. Fortunately, our intentions were arrested by a shout of triumph, and we turned and saw that one of the men had succeeded in smashing the lock of the gate with a bullet, and the way behind it stood open. We swarmed through and so gained a temporary respite from the hail of lead behind us.

We, the remnants of that fine company which had so gaily entered the grounds of that convent less than twenty-four hours previously, now left it, swamped by feelings of a far different and melancholy nature, and proceeded to create, as rapidly as possible, a great open space between us and the enemy.

With this end in view, we took the direction of a road that ran obliquely to the right towards a ridge, the crest of which was about eight hundred yards farther away.

We all kept together in a bunch for a while. The unsoundness of proceeding in this manner entered into my mind. I considered that our very numbers would at once attract the attention of the roving eye of the 'Boche', as soon as he came clear of the wall of the convent behind us; whereas, by splitting up into smaller numbers, it might be possible to avoid any unwelcome unpleasantenss of this sort. I mentioned the outcome of my reflections to a sergeant of my company named Morris, who heartily concurred, with the result that the pair of us left the bulk and struck off on a line of our own selection, choosing a much shorter route to the top of the ridge, which led directly across cultivated fields.

We plodded along, alternately running and walking quite merrily, for a while unmolested, with the going fairly heavy and uphill, quite happy in our choice.

A vicious whispering sort of noise about our ears, warned us that something had gone awry with our clever ideas, and that we had been spotted and were objects of great interest to our 'friends', the 'Boche'. Filled with misgiving and disgust, we did the only thing possible under the circumstances, and threw ourselves flat upon the ground, playing 'possum' in the hope of inducing the enemy to believe that we were no longer worth his trouble.

The ruse was successful, and his fire abated, and when we were rested we decided to carry on.

We accordingly rose and moved onward, progressing as speedily as possible. After a time we again became the object of the enemy's attention, and, amid the evidences of his affection for us, we found that our forward movement was temporarily arrested by a barbed wire fence.

In attempting to negotiate this obstacle, the pack upon my back became wedged between the strands of wire, securing me a prisoner, and defying all my efforts to effect my release.

I hung there, dangling helplessly, a fact the enemy took the utmost advantage of, as evidenced by the storm of wasp-like noises that filled the air around me. In dreadful suspense, expecting momentarily to feel the thud of the impact of a bullet on my body, I struggled for freedom, without avail.

Sergeant Morris had thrown himself down in a more or less sheltered spot, about fifty yards ahead. Discovering my absence from his side, he glanced around and perceived my predicament. Without a single thought for his own safety, in spite of the very brisk fire that was being directed all about me, rendering his chances of approaching me and remaining unscathed exceedingly remote, he sprang up and dashed to my assistance.

Finding it difficult to disentangle my pack from the wire, he pulled out his jack-knife and coolly cut it from me, and, leaving it hanging abandoned on the fence, we both hurriedly crawled to a slight depression and flattened out.

The only award my good friend the gallant sergeant ever received for that exhibition of bravery and unselfishness was my heartfelt and grateful thanks.

All signs of firing having again ceased, we resumed our struggle towards our objective for quite a considerable distance, without further interference, until, arriving at a comfortable and roomy fold in the ground, we took advantage of the cover it offered to secure a refresher and regain our breath.

Whilst lying here I ventured an opinion that everything that happened in life was for the best, I referred to the incident of the barbed wire as a good example. At first I had cause to curse its action in holding me, to my intense discomfort, exposed to the enemy's fire, but since I had discovered a reason to recognise that it possessed its beneficent influence, for it had relieved me of the painful necessity of bearing about on my shoulders nearly a hundredweight of equipment.

The attention of my companion being drawn, by my remarks, to a means of securing ease and relief from a long-suffered burden, he asked me to relieve him of an overbearing tyrant without further delay, and I hastened to remove his pack, which, after removing from its interior a few treasured articles, he discarded.

These adjustments had taken some little time, and at the conclusion of them, we, being fully rested, decided to get along once again. We started to rise to carry out this project, but before we had an opportunity to reach an erect position a perfect tornado of shots sent us thudding violently back to earth.

We stared at each other in horrified consternation, for this fusillade had come from the direction of the crest of the very hill we had been struggling so hard to reach.

Taking a pessimistic view, we decided that we had become surrounded and cut off by the enemy.

The speed in which he had accomplished this operation was marvellous, and filled us with amazement, which was so great that we began to consider it an impossibility. There was no doubt, however, that the shots had come from the hill, and if the enemy had not had time to get into that position, then there must have been a misunderstanding. With a faint hope that this was indeed the case, we tried it out by placing our hats on our rifles and waving them aloft.

'For the love of Mike, if it's not lying dead ye are at this blessed minute, thin tell me, who might ye be?' bawled an unmistakably Irish voice, which fell upon our ears like heavenly music, and was so welcomely re-assuring that, without more ado, we sprang up and made ourselves known.

Hastily scrambling up and joining these murder-ously-inclined friends, we found that they were part of the Royal Irish Regiment, one of the battalions composing our brigade.

They had taken up position at the top of the ridge while we were sheltering in the hollow beneath. As they did not expect to see any but enemy troops turn up on their front, they did not waste time in con-sidering the uniform we wore before opening their fire on us on our sudden and surprising appearance.

'It's entirely the bad shooting of these blackguards that you've to thank for being here,' explained an officer in a decidedly aggrieved tone, 'for it's no credit to them that ye're both not lying dead below.'

As for us, we accepted this very doubtful expres-sion of congratulation at our escape with heartfelt thanks.

We remained chatting to these Irishmen, giving them most harrowing descriptions of the nature of the attacks they were likely to experience if they stayed long enough, which could not have improved their morale in any way.

These tales, happily for the peace of mind of these gullible sons of Erin, were cut short by the arrival on the spot of the remainder of my company. On exchanging notes, the sergeant and I found that the tactics we had employed must have been entirely wrong, judging from the experience of the remainder; for, whereas we had been subjected to fire during practically the whole of our journey, they had not been worried by a single shot. The relation of our unpleasant ordeal brought us a good deal of chaffing.

At this place we checked up our numbers, which were found to make up the melancholy total of one officer and seventy odd other ranks, the residue of six officers and two hundred and fifty odd other ranks who had composed the company when we went into action that morning.

On completing this discouraging tally, we sadly moved off in an endeavour to find the remainder of our shattered battalion.

While proceeding upon our search we passed numerous fresh troops moving up to take up positions from which to resist the enemy's advance. The passage of us war-tried veterans excited their curiosity and attention, for they had not, up to that moment, been under fire or within sight of the foe.

With our first engagement had passed our original pristine smartness, and our uniform was, for the most part, torn and soiled almost beyond recognition, and quite a lot of our equipment, deemed by us to be entirely superfluous, was missing from about our persons.

We were saluted during our passage by these troops with a great deal of witty badinage, which amused us immensely, and served to shake us out of the despondency into which we had fallen and to restore us to a more normal frame of mind.

We magnanimously forebore to say the things to them that might have hurt their feelings, for we knew that they had yet to undergo an experience that would tend to damp their comical inclinations, and we contented ourselves by passing them and their sallies with smiles of knowing and pitying contempt for their ignorance. Many miles we tramped upon our quest, making many an inquiry in endeavours to locate the whereabouts of the battalion, without success, so that we began to imagine that we, alone, were the sole survivors of that unit, and as it was growing dark it was decided to select a position in which to pass the night. We were, at this time, a little to the south, and to the west of Mons, having avoided this town during our travels of that day.

About to examine the defensive possibilities of a small hill, we were accosted by a mounted officer, who, to our surprise and relief, proved to be our own Commanding Officer, who gave us the very glad news that the remainder of our battalion, numbering about three hundred men, were resting in a field further along the the road; we followed him and joined them. Never will I be able to forget the remarkable scenes that attended this reunion.

Men of all ages threw themselves frenziedly into each other's arms, swearing, shouting, and capering about in the wildest transports of joy.—How unemotional Britishers really are!

For my part, I was filled with a great anxiety respecting the fate of my young and only brother, who was serving in another company of the battalion as a stretcher-bearer.

Possessed with a fear of receiving bad news, occasioned by the vivid remembrance of the scene of that morning in which other British stretcher-bearers played the chief rôle, I refrained from asking questions, scared by the possibilities of the replies, and contented myself with moving in and out of the milling mob, in the hope of finding him.

I had just about seen everybody except the object of my search, and had concluded that he was to be numbered among the missing, when I perceived one of the most pleasant sights of my life.

We caught a glimpse of each other at the identical moment. I gathered that he had been pursuing a similar quest, consumed by the same concern regarding me, for he was taking no part in the mad revels, but was standing alone, anxiously scanning the crowd. Controlling my emotions of relief and pleasure, I permitted myself to drift slowly towards him, and when near enough, said quite casually:

'Hullo! Len, all right?' to which he replied with an air of equal unconcern:

'Yes! are you?'

'Oh quite, thanks!' I added, and we each continued on our ways, each acting as though the other was less than nothing at all to him. Peculiar is the nature of brothers.

I was almost overwhelmed with a desire to throw my arms around his neck, and cry and cry like hell, I was so happy to see him safe and well. I am sure he was possessed of precisely the same feelings towards me.

A pathetic scene was witnessed as the battalion was paraded for Roll Call.

Extraordinary and inexplicable emotions swept us, as name after name was called, eliciting nothing but a deathly, ominous silence. Imagination ran riot. What and where were the absentees who on that morning had been happy, cheerful men, full of boisterous health and good humour?

A sight of that well-known picture, *The Roll Call*, by Lady Butler, always brings the scene of that night clearly before me.

We stood there in similar broken ranks, many swathed in bandages, soberly listening to the grim tally of the cost to us of that day's fighting.

The sum represented an expenditure of six hundred and seventy odd officers and men from an original total of just over one thousand and fifty.

Of the company that had occupied the railway station, there was not one single representative. Ninety per cent. of the casualties had been inflicted alone by the German artillery, against which at that time we had an absurdly inadequate reply.

The Commanding Officer succeeded in raising our spirits by the delivery of a kindly speech, in which he told us, in no uncertain terms, that we had acquitted ourselves like good soldiers and men, in this, our first experience of War, and that he was exceedingly proud

of us. He laid stress on the point that, although we had
been compelled to fall back, that move had been according to the plan laid down, as the impossibility of
holding on without complete extermination in the face
of overwhelming bodies of the enemy was recognised,
as we had no other troops available to support us.

He went on to inform us that for the next few days
we would be called upon to face that most difficult and
hazardous of all operations of War, namely, a planned
and organised retreat.

We were adjured not to allow the constantly retard-
ing action, with all the hardships it entailed, to cause
us any uneasiness or dismay, for the day would surely
come when we would receive a good opportunity to
reverse the movement. When that occasion arrived
we would, no doubt, discover that the enemy would
fail to acquit himself under similiar circumstances as
well as we had done. This homily bucked us up wonderfully, and, almost cheerfully, we set to work to
entrench ourselves, and to prepare ourselves against
surprise for the night.

CHAPTER XI

Having completed our defence works, we looked around for something that would stave off the cravings of our inner men.

Napoleon had said that an army fights and marches on its stomach.

We certainly looked like being compelled to do that very thing, through lack of strength to carry out the necessary manœuvres standing on our feet, if the food supply was going to continue to remain as conspicuous by its absence as it was at this time.

The only edible articles we found in our vicinity were the horses drawing our ammunition supplies, which had, in some miraculous manner, managed to cling to us.

They were not of much further use, as the carts had been denuded of their contents by the demand made upon them by us in replenishing ammunition pouches.

My thoughts flashed to my old friend the company cook, and I began to nurse his memory with an almost loving regard. I wondered how he had fared, and I remembered, with a forgiving spirit, that he had always 'fared' very badly, but my thoughts were really concerned at that moment with his welfare.

Had he turned up this night he would have been accorded a welcome, in spite of all his faults, that would have caused the father of the Prodigal Son to consume his beard with envy, and his vilest output would have been treated with the respect usually reserved for the nectar of the gods.

With a sad sigh of remorse at the memory of all the harsh feelings I had entertained for him, I tightened my belt and resignedly chewed some grass.

When it had grown dark, shells could be observed bursting over the neighbourhood of the town of Mons, while, now and again, the sounds of heavy musketry fire could be heard, signifying that the contending forces were still more or less actively engaged.

The result of the preponderance of the enemy's artillery was a sore blow to us. We felt positive, from the knowledge acquired by our personal experience, that in action in which infantry were opposed by infantry alone, we would always render a very good account of ourselves, even if the enemy were many times in numbers the stronger. This was not in any way considered boastfully, as it was proved to be the truth time after time.

The employment of artillery against us gave us no chance, and rendered us impotent, an aspect which gave us but little encouragement.

Being thoroughly exhausted we dozed off uncomfortably in fits and starts.

We were suddenly jerked into a wakeful state of alarm by the hoarse challenges of our outpost sentries.

Approaching sounds, giving every indication of the advance of hordes of cavalry, caused us hurriedly to load our rifles and to 'stand to' in readiness to repel an assault.

Arrested by the shouts of our guards, the cavalcade came to a halt, and immediately the air was pierced by the frightened screams and cries of women and children.

I went forward with a reconnoitring party, and, on arriving at the scene of the clamour, discovered a train of miserable refugees, most of whom were kneeling in the road, praying feverishly.

Carts and wagons, drawn by a weird assortment of animals, were heaped up with all the goods and chattels they had been able to hastily pile into them before being caught and arrested by the enemy advance.

They presented one of the most heart-breaking sights it is possible to witness, and their relief was as great as our own when identities were established.

The poor devils thought that they had blundered right into the enemy, on hearing our challenges, delivered in what was, to them, a foreign tongue, and indeed they had a narrow escape from being shot down, as our sentries, not being understood, and consequently failing to receive a reply to their challenges, were about to open fire, and only the timely and unexpected screams of the scared women arrested their intentions.

These unfortunate people were travelling to the rear in the search for safety, somewhat belatedly.

The officer in command of our party advised them to make for the French coast with all possible speed,

M

and, in all probability, they eventually found sanctuary in England.

We passed them along on their sad pilgrimage with many expressions of good will for their safe journey.

Interruptions of a similar nature continued at intervals throughout the whole time we remained in this position. That we were unable to secure them against this miserable experience, by providing a barrier against the enemy advance, filled us with remorse.

Early in the morning, just before the dawn, a slight contretemps occurred which resulted in the loss of two perfectly innocent and gentle lives.

One of the sentinels, peering into the gloom, suddenly espied figures stealthily moving in his direction. Failing to elicit a response to his challenges, he opened fire, the sound of his outburst creating the wildest excitement and apprehension in the camp.

The discovery of the corpses of two cows testified to the watchfulness of our guard, and we relaxed our excited vigilance with expressions of relief.

When daylight enabled us to look round, I sought a view of these unfortunate victims of circumstances, and was forced to rub my eyes and pinch myself at the peculiar sight they presented.

It appeared that the bullets of that sentry had possessed the uncanny and unusual power of flaying the beasts and removing the greater part of the flesh thus exposed.

I rightly guessed, after reflection, that some of the starving men had felt too hungry to allow such a unique gift of food to go begging.

Daylight found me absolutely raging with hunger, and I eagerly watched for signs that would reveal to me the identity of the 'butchers', in the hope of being able to secure a titbit to allay the pangs of emptiness that assailed me, but all in vain, and I surmised that they must have devoured the meat raw and warm as they hacked it away from the carcasses.

A large farmhouse lay a short distance in front of us, and on the pretext of obtaining drinking water I sought permission to take a party to it, which was granted.

To our great disappointment, it was found deserted, and the most minute search failed to reveal anything in the nature of food. This almost broke our hearts, and we returned miserably to our unit.

I ventured to ask my company commander if there was any chance of our field kitchens turning up. He gravely informed me that they had 'turned up', having been blown to splinters, together with the whole of the remainder of our transport. Nothing can repress the funny streak running in some people.

At about 9 a.m. we saw a large body of our troops advancing from our rear, forming a spectacle that must have caused the enemy artillery to hug themselves with huge delight.

This bold column must have mistaken the War for an advertising campaign, with a kind of 'join the army and see the world and get a good chance to forget it' motive behind it.

They came up smartly, with their rifles at the slope, bayonets fixed and twinkling prettily in the morning sun, acting like a bunch of heliographs, flashing the good news of their presence to the enemy. These 'bright' soldiers halted on our left flank and, with a great display of energy possessing an aggravating kind of ' we'll show you how to do it ' air, prepared to dig in.

At this activity our commander, very war-wise, advanced us to a position about two hundred and fifty yards ahead. Looking back from here at the toilers we had left behind, we interestedly concentrated our attention on their precise methods of arranging positions for defence.

Non-commissioned officers rushed about laying large marking tapes, which were meticulously aligned. When this part of the operation had been completed successfully to their satisfaction, the men were lined up along these tapes, each being spaced at equal distances apart, measured to within an inch.

Everything being ready, the thing fully expected by us happened, and the War, which had apparently forgotten us during the last few hours, re-opened again with great vigour, as the shells, that had practically been invited, paid their visits to the new line about to be constructed.

The tactics of our commanding officer had placed us beyond the immediate attention of these unwelcome callers, and we had leisure to observe the result of the havoc they created in the lines of the battalion in our rear, with great pity. We were glad to see that they did not scorn to benefit by our experience, as they soon grasped the sound sense and reason of our strategy, and came up discreetly alongside of us, forming, no doubt, a resolution to carry themselves more modestly in the future.

Additional troops came up into line on our right and left flanks, and we presented an unbroken front towards the expected onslaught of the enemy.

In due course, his infantry appeared and we compelled him to deploy and engage us.

Finding it impossible to make progress against us, he patiently waited for his artillery to accomplish the job the infantry miserably failed to do.

They obliged with a deadly accuracy, which blew us from our frail defences, and forced us to retire, but not before we had hung on so long that it was almost too late, and we found ourselves almost surrounded, and a desperate rear-guard action took place as we endeavoured to cut our way out.

Considerably reduced in numbers, we at last succeeded in clearing a passage and shaking off our would-be captors. Before this had been successfully accomplished we had spent considerable time and covered a great deal of country, which caused us to lose touch with our main body.

A new phase of fighting thus commenced for us, fraught with the utmost peril, for we were alone and entirely unsupported.

In a country teeming with overwhelming bodies of the enemy, we became a sort of flying patrol, if dragging a foot, bloody and raw, encased in a number ten sized boot that appeared to weigh a ton, can be, by any stretch of imagination, considered flying. We marched and counter-marched any distance for one, or several miles, in our endeavours to elude the foe, and regain the rest of our Brigade. We carried on until our progress in that particular direction was arrested by the sight of the enemy. If his strength warranted it, we engaged him in a little private war of our own. If, on the other hand, he appeared in too great a number to be overcome, we remembered that discretion was the better part of valour, and withdrew to try our luck elsewhere. The game was proceeded with after the style of 'here we come gathering nuts in May', except that we had more desire to give the 'nuts' than to receive them, being firm believers in the knowledge that it was certainly more blessed to give, etc.

One boon granted us during these operations brought us great solace; it was the discovery that we were not being favoured by the attentions of the enemy artillery.

Our chief source of peril came from wandering bands of Uhlans, which were following close on the line of retreat.

These snapped up any straggler who had found it impossible, either through the effects of severe wounds or other exhaustion, to keep up with his unit.

We had, during the course of our wanderings this day, encountered, and successfully disposed of, three different patrols of these ubique cavalrymen when we almost stumbled into an ambush.

Our first warning of danger came with a startling volley, which placed shots into us, wounding and

dropping three of our force. Dashing towards anything that offered protection or cover from these un-
seen attackers, we searched the country anxiously, and
were rewarded by the sight of a small body of Uhlans
galloping furiously away from us, they having emerged
from concealment behind a thicket standing about
three hundred yards from our right flank. We speeded
them on their way with a scattered volley, and the
commanding officer decided to take advantage of an
eminence in the shape of a small tower, part of a
deserted farmhouse, to effect a reconnaissance before
proceeding on our way.

A couple of officers mounted and became the centre
of our interest, as they closely subjected the neigh-
bouring country to a scrutiny through powerful field-
glasses.

I suddenly saw, by their excited attitude, that they
had observed something of note, and one of them
hastily descended and anxiously conferred with the
commanding officer, who returned with him to the
tower.

A rapid glance in the direction pointed out by his
informant apparently enabled him to form his deci-
sions, for he came down and issued orders which
resulted in us assuming positions of defence about the
farm. We were told to watch for a considerable force of
enemy cavalry that were aproaching with the obvious
intention of attacking our small company. The party
that had fired upon us a few minutes previously had
evidently been scouting in advance of their main body,
and their information as to our scanty numbers had

probably influenced their commander to try conclusions with us. He had a lot to learn, had that
commander.

The tactics they observed in approaching us were
highly commendable, up to a point, for they were
using a small wood, about two hundred yards from
our position, to cover their advance, and they would
have doubtless taken us completely by surprise,
whilst exposed in the open, had it not been for the
sagacity displayed by our commander in instituting
the precautionary measure of examining our surroundings after the preliminary attack made on us,
before proceeding further. Their appearance from this
wood furnished the majority of us with our first
glimpse of them. They came sweeping out towards us
in a compact body about four hundred strong, travelling like the wind, crouched forward on their
chargers, with lances levelled in a business-like attitude. Really an awe-inspiring and magnificent spectacle.

We opened fire, and momentarily checked the swift
advance, but they were rallied, and proceeded towards
us with renewed vigour. Suddenly they were lost to our
view as they disappeared into a small valley, or rather,
deep depression in the ground about eighty yards from
our front.

Immediately we were ordered to hold our fire and to
concentrate and wait for their re-appearance on the
lip of the depression nearest to us. The instant they
appeared they received the full force of the terrific
blast of fire that was directed by us upon them.

That proved the end of a perfect day for most of them, as they were literally blown back into the hollow. None gained our side of that small valley and remained there alive. The survivors gamely engaged us in a musketry duel, which inflicted several nasty casualties upon us, but this was undertaken apparently to keep our attention occupied in that direction, a ruse that was almost, but not entirely, successful.

A body of cavalry unexpectedly issued from each end of this valley, and simultaneously attacked us on each flank. With a murderous fire we endeavoured to stop their rush, but fully thirty of them succeeded in leaping the wall of our defences on one flank, and in subjecting us to a harassing attack upon our rear.

The seriousness of the situation was only relieved when the men protecting the other flank, having successfully repelled the attack made upon them, were able to add their efforts to the subjugating of these bold invaders.

No quarter was given or received, and these gallant Uhlans died to a man, but not without us paying a stiff price for our victory.

The enemy forming, no doubt, a conclusion that we offered too tough a proposition for him to contend with successfully alone, dashed out from the shelter of the valley, in retirement towards the wood.

Upon this we reconnoitred the valley and the ground surrounding our position, where we found numerous dead and wounded men and horses. The tally showed that this attack had cost the enemy losses amounting to over forty dead and sixty odd wounded, who were found actually lying abandoned on the ground.

We suffered twenty-one killed and thirteen wounded. All the horses too badly injured to recover were mercifully relieved of their agony, while the others were commandeered to carry our own wounded.

The enemy wounded were all carried into the shelter of the farmhouse, where, after having been relieved of their arms, they were left to tend each other as well as possible until their compatriots should arrive. It was impossible for us to burden ourselves with prisoners of war in our situation.

A sudden discovery was made that these troops were each in possession of an ample supply of appetising looking food.

The necessities of war and our empty bellies compelled us to attach these welcome supplies, and we grimly removed every scrap from these unwilling contributors to our commissariat.

We subsequently feasted royally on hunks of bread, covered generously with a succulent sort of potted pork, being not at all deterred or concerned by the angry scowls our late foemen bestowed upon our gastronomic exercises.

Concluding our repast we solemnly buried our dead, erecting a monument about them composed of the ruined and smashed arms captured from the enemy.

An incident now occurred which decided our commanding officer to make an immediate move from the scene of this action. A humming noise, that I first attributed to the distant approach of a shell, made itself heard, and a sudden exclamation drew our attention to the sky, where an aeroplane could be observed coming towards us. Immediately reference to our pamphlets gave us the information that it was a German 'Taube', looking very much like a large and graceful eagle with its birdlike wings and tail.

We awaited his arrival, determined to bring him down, but on spotting us before actually crossing above us, the pilot gracefully banked, and, executing a derisive gesture with his hand, turned and sped swiftly away. We followed his example, and made great haste to get far away from that farm in the shortest time possible.

We had marched for about two hours, and, on completing a climb up a hill, halted to rest a few minutes on the top. Away in the valley below us on the side towards which we were travelling, lay an immense forest, oblong in shape, one end being approximately opposite to the spot were we lay resting.

A gasp of incredulous amazement focussed our eyes on a sight which thrilled me to the very marrow.

Two bodies of mounted men were converging upon the point which formed the apex of the rectangle at the lower right hand corner of the forest opposite, the distance from us lending them a toylike appearance.

Field glasses were anxiously concentrated on these bodies, and it was ascertained that the party moving down on the right towards the point were British, and the others, moving across our front, were German troops. Each appeared to be entirely oblivious to the presence of the other. We were thrown into paroxysms of agony and suspense as we waited for that soul thrilling drama to unfold. Men madly shrieked out cries of warning to our cavalrymen, rendered unavailing by the distance intervening between us. Then a great sob-strangled silence descended upon us as the climax was reached.

Our men turned the corner and projected themselves on to the startled visions of their opponents.

I saw the 'Boche' instinctively draw rein and hesitate. Not so the British. I fancied I heard a roar, as I saw them plunge forward without the slightest hesitation, their swords flashing brightly as they whipped them from their scabbards.

Into and through that shrinking body of Germans they surged, their blades twinkling merrily in the sunlight as they furiously cut down their opponents, who were apparently paralysed and rendered helpless by the shock of surprise. The tremendous vigour of the British attack immediately reduced the enemy to a flying, disorganised rabble, of which our men took the utmost advantage, pursuing and cutting them down with great *élan* whenever opportunity presented itself, continuing to harass the enemy and drive home the lesson, until they all disappeared from our ken.

We stood on that hill, cheering, dancing and raving like madmen at this wonderful feat of our countrymen.

The sight of these British troopers was also inspiring from the point of view that it was evidence that we were nearing the vicinity of our army.

We were now in the neighbourhood of a small village, which we approached with great care.

On entering it we found it deserted by most of the usual inhabitants, but in the road running through it, was a convoy of motor transport, part of a British ammunition train. At first we thought the lorries abandoned, as we went up to them without being challenged in any way.

On closer inspection, however, we found two men on each driving seat sleeping as soundly and unconcernedly as though they were employed on a moving job in the neighbourhood of Wapping.

A couple of wags donned German helmets they had secured as trophies, poked their heads over the breast-work screen the drivers had erected in front of their seat, and emitted horrible grunting noises.

The sleepers came awake, and with eyes popping out like organ stops at the apparitions confronting them, grabbed for their rifles, whereupon the jokers, anxious to forestall any untimely misunderstanding and accident, revealed their identity.

The lorries were found to be packed with supplies of ammunition of all sorts, and our commanding officer immediately took advantage of these to replenish our depleted stocks. The advisability of unloading this stuff and replacing it by ourselves, was gravely debated among the officers, but, to our chagrin, was decided against, the decision being mostly influenced by the information extracted from the Army Service Corps men that they had been part of a column attached to a division that had halted in this village at three o'clock that afternoon.

They could not give any explanation for the reason they had been left behind, as they had fallen asleep almost immediately upon stopping, having been without rest for days. As it was now about half past seven in the evening, we had reason to expect that, with luck, we would quickly catch up with the body of troops that had passed through this village a short time previously. The presentation to these men of the information that they were almost surrounded by enemy troops and that we had only just emerged from an engagement that had taken place within the last few miles, produced in them signs of marvellous activity, and they cleared from that village, not standing on the order of their going, and disappeared from our sight, amid clouds of dust.

Dusk was falling, and having decided our route, the commanding officer decided to keep on the move all night in an endeavour to link up with our main body, as the slightest delay would probably involve our extinction or capture.

Throwing out a screen of skirmishers we continued cautiously, feeling our way through a night filled with excursions and alarms, to daylight.

Shortly after dawn had broken a sight was revealed to our happy, but intensely weary eyes. A few hundred yards away we observed British troops in strong numbers actively engaged in preparing positions, the rear of which spelt comparative safety, and probably food and rest, to us.

We cautiously approached, seeking by every means to make our nationality evident, and to eliminate any risk of mistake in our identity that would draw upon us unmerited chastisement from these, our friends.

Thus had our commanding officer succeeded in extricating us from our unenviable position, and ably guided and restored us to the arms of our army.

CHAPTER XII

Among the troops we joined we found survivors of our own brigade, who had all experienced a very trying time, and were almost as exhausted as we were owing to lack of sleep and rest.

Our fond dreams of obtaining a period of tranquil ease and sleep were rudely torn from us when we were instructed to assist in the completion of these new defence works. I quite realised that it was only the sheer necessity of war that compelled our commanders to set us to this heart-breaking task in the hopelessly fatigued condition to which we were reduced.

Men dropped in their tracks while working, fast asleep, and were only aroused to resume their labours by the application of the most strenuous efforts on the part of the officers who, of course, were quite as worn-out as we were.

We were told that it was imperative for us to delay the enemy as long as possible, to enable fresh divisions to get into position in our rear. When this had been accomplished we would be able to secure our much-needed rest.

The mode of operation that it was proposed to adopt was carefully explained to us. We were told to hold on till the last minute, then, on receipt of the order, every man, acting for himself, would retire and continue to retire as fast as possible, through another line of troops waiting in position behind us, until his further progress was arrested by officers specially detailed for that duty.

We, having completed our digging, flopped into the results of our handiwork, and without more ado collapsed into a dreamless and deep slumber.

Concussions and the sounds of hideous explosions aroused me to a hellish realisation that we were in the thick of things once more, and I, with the others, scrambled into a position from whence I could deliver the best account of myself, absolutely dazed, to a point verging on unconsciousness, by the effects of the sleepless period through which we had passed.

I was reduced to such a pitiful physical condition that I did not care what happened to me, and almost welcomed the thought of a blow that would end this awful distress and agony of mind.

I deduced from a weary glance at my neighbours that their ideas and sensations were practically the same. A ragged, dirty-looking crew, whose eyes appeared, and had as much expression, as oysters floating in a plate of gravy.

Even as the shells fell about us we dozed fitfully, evincing as much interest in them as we would have regarded bursting air balloons, the men wounded by the bursts appearing too tired to mention the matter.

The eventual appearance on the scene of the enemy infantry aroused us to a certain extent, and we continued the engagement until the receipt of the order to retire.

Getting up and stumbling blindly, like a lot of
drunken men, we left the trenches, containing their
burden of those who had obtained their release from
the grind, and proceeded, guided by sheer instinct
alone, to our rear.

Returning to consciousness momentarily on the way,
I discovered my young brother by my side, and,
linking arms for mutual assistance, we proceeded in
silence without a word until, after passing through the
expected line, we were gathered up to join the other
stragglers who had successfully filtered through.

When it was considered that the last of the pitiful
remnants of the brigade that were likely still to be active had turned up, we continued in column of route,
through a second line of troops, and beyond them for
about a further three miles, where we were kindly
invited to dig again.

It would be impossible to gain any idea of the enormity of the suffering that can be inflicted upon a
person by continually depriving him of his sleep, without actual experience.

I should imagine that it is one of the most damnable
tortures ever devised.

On completing our work here, however, we were
permitted to enjoy nearly five hours of uninterrupted
sleep, which recuperated us to remarkable degree.

The now usual burst and subsequent din of exploding
shells, served as our reveille, but this time we assumed
our defensive positions with an alertness that con-
trasted very favourably with our demeanour of five
hours previously.

It was during the hottest part of this particular action, while we were actually under intense enemy artillery and musketry fire, that an incident occurred worthy of the highest commendation, the central figure being an heroine, an aged French woman.

In our trench were lying several badly wounded men pleading for a drink, which we were unable to give them as all our supplies had been consumed.

One good soldier gallantly volunteered to make his hazardous way to a little cottage that could be seen about three hundred yards behind us, to procure some water to alleviate their distress.

On being granted permission to make the attempt, he blithely gathered as many water bottles as he could conveniently carry and set off on his errand of mercy.

Imagine my intense surprise when I saw him returning unconcernedly towards us bearing two buckets in addition to the water bottles, which were hanging in festoons about his neck and shoulders, accompanied by a feminine figure similarly burdened.

Only my clenched teeth prevented my heart from getting all messed up in the dirt of the trench, as I, almost bursting with indescribable suspense, watched their leisurely approach.

Hardly able to credit the evidence of my senses, they arrived at our trench unscathed, and the brave lady proudly stood, exposed to the full fury of the enemy fire, at the brink of the trench, her russet face wrinkled with a motherly smile, until half-a-dozen of the men sprang out to her and bundled her into the questionable safety of the trench.

Here, with queer clucking noises of intense sympathy,
she administered to the comfort of the wounded, with
all the fuss attendant on the actions of an old hen with
her brood.

As she observed the injuries suffered by these men
her dear old eyes became clouded with pain and tears,
as she tore her petticoat to pieces to supplement the
rude bandages that had already been applied.

She was quite sixty-five years old, and the man she
had accompanied was full of remorse at not being
able to prevent her attempting her risky venture, and
had not been aware that she had intended to accompany him until he had discovered her presence when
half way on his return journey.

He had been nonplussed by her action, but had
wisely decided not to expose her to more danger than
necessary, by attempting to enter into any argument
that would have been rendered futile by their mutual
ignorance of one another's language.

Her presence filled us with emotion, and I saw
several tough-looking men approach her and shyly lay
their hands lightly upon her shoulders, in a caress of
homage and respect for her noble courage.

Those nearest her constituted themselves her shield
and bodyguard from the metal hurtling around, for
as a shell burst on the brink of the spot on which she
knelt performing her compassionate actions, they
threw themselves over her, two of them receiving
wounds in the process.

At this, she broke into loud exclamations, seemingly
expostulating against this sacrifice, for she smiled

sweetly the whole time, and on the incident being repeated, she, without any warning, climbed out of the trench and wended her way back to her cottage, shaking her head gravely, apparently at the troubled reflection that by her presence in the firing line she had been the cause of a lot of unnecessary anxiety.

With what dismay and feelings of terrible apprehension we watched her progress.

She was, indeed, beloved of the gods, for with tremendous relief we saw her reach and disappear into her humble home without being scratched. Truly a miracle.

We were compelled, eventually, by sheer necessity, to repeat our former tactics and retire.

I passed quite close to the old lady's house, and saw her standing, looking out of the window. She waved encouragingly at us as we passed, in a way that filled my eyes with tears, as I thought of her being left alone to face the ruthless hordes of enemy soldiery following close upon us.

The retreat had now become thoroughly organised, and the whole job was performed in a thoroughly business-like manner, which heartened us considerably, and we carried out the intentions of our commanders with great *élan*.

Sometimes our defences would delay the enemy advance for hours, greatly to his annoyance and decided inconvenience, as it gave the troops that had passed through to the rear, great opportunities for rest and consequent recovery from fatigue.

Further evidence that the retreat was under perfect control was supplied at the appearance, at cross-roads, etc., of sign-posts bearing directions of all the routes to be followed to effect connection with the various units.

There were also, at selected points, dumps of ammunition, placed conveniently to enable every man to keep himself fully supplied as necessity demanded.

During one of our quiet spells whilst proceeding in our game of 'leap-frog' to a new position, we had just left the precincts of a village when an expensive-looking car approached from the direction in which we were headed and pulled up alongside of us.

It contained two dust-covered occupants, and a voice with an unmistakable accent, bawled:

'Say you, Guys! have you seen anything of this 'lil War?'

'Seen the War, old Cock?' queried one of our cockney wits; 'What the bleedin' 'ell mikes yer fink we've seen the War? Corse we've not, we've bin aht pickin' disys fer muvver ter mike chines wiv.'

'I'm sorry, soldier, I certainly didn't intend to annoy you in any way. Believe me, boys, I've been chasing around all over France to get a peep at this War. I'll feel very much obliged to you if you will tell me where I'd be most likely to find it!' apologised the motorist.

'And I s'pose if you likes it, you'll buy it! If you reely wants to see it, tike my advice and 'op aht uv that blinkin' 'ortermobeel and tike the choob to the next tarn: when yer gets there 'op aht at the 'igh Street, tike the first to the right, and you'll find the War darn

the second turnin' on the left,' volunteered our spokes-
man, maintaining the whole time the solemn air of a
judge.

'You're hellfired crazy!' shouted our cousin from
'God's own country' as he fiercely let in his clutch
and commenced to move away in high dudgeon.

'I figure to find it without your aid, stranger.'

'I figger yer'll be obliged ter, folks!' mimicked our
irrepressible cockney. The departing victims of his
caustic wit having hurriedly placed themselves beyond
his reach, he directed his concluding remarks at us,
saying:

'Them blokes carn't kid me they're lookin' fer a war!
It's a couple of little golding 'arps they're 'untin' for!'

This interchange of courtesies put us into the highest
humour, and we continued, alternately marching and
fighting all the day.

Towards the evening a terrific thunder-storm broke
over the country, appearing like a majestic gesture of
the Almighty's disapproval of this senseless rapine and
slaughter. The whole atmosphere was enveloped in
sudden gloom, followed by a deluge that was nothing
short of a cloudburst, drenching us to the skin, but
certainly not doing us any harm, on the contrary,
proving most beneficial, as we could readily observe
from the cleanly improvement in the faces of each other.

While this storm was at its height we entered a town
where we were invited to take shelter by the inhabitants.

I found myself with half a dozen others in a large
room of a house. Standing right opposite us as we were

ushered in, was a large mirror which captured our reflections.

The apparitions we saw therein claimed our fascinated attention. I was particularly struck by the presence of one unfamiliar and unpleasant-looking face among the group which I failed to recognise, and I turned away and looked among my colleagues to see who this stranger might be, but I could not find him. On raising my hand to my face I observed this scarecrow duplicate the action; it was then, to my intense horror, that I discovered I was responsible for the presence of this disgusting image.

All had evidently received a similar shock, and we went forward and crowded round the glass, fingering our unsightly beards, and other disfigurements with gasps of surprised awe.

Four young women came into the room and stood observing our antics with smiles of pity for our sorry looks. They moved around us, feeling our drenched clothing with charming concern. The eldest looking woman addressed some remarks to the others which caused them all to retire for a couple of minutes, and then one of them returned and smilingly beckoned us to follow her. She led us to a delightfully comfortable looking kitchen, in which was a large and cheerful fire, standing in the centre of a group of chairs that had been thoughtfully arranged around it.

We then received signs from her, indicating that she desired us to remove our tunics, which she then collected and hung about the room to dry.

While she was performing this kindly office, the others arrived bearing heaps of clean linen.

They conveyed to us, by pantomime, that they expected us to take off our shirts. This, we thought, a bit tall, and we gazed at each other coyly. They redoubled their gestures, supplementing them by the frequent mention of the immodest word of 'chemise', which overwhelmed us with bashfulness.

Fearing that our lack of activity to comply with their desires was due to our failure to understand the nature of the action required of us, one of the damsels came over to me and began to remove my shirt.

I started to remonstrate, but as the sensation was not unpleasant, I permitted her to perform this service amid the outraged, but slightly envious, glances and schoolgirl-like giggles of my companions.

This operation concluded, my fair tormenter gave me a clean, dry, sweet-smelling garment. It was the most extraordinary shirt I have ever laid eyes on.

It was as glorious as a coat of arms, being made of linen, stiffened by the application of much starch, of colour—ground verdant, with rings circling, or, and collar distinctly rampant.

The startling change wrought in my appearance by this work of art drew forth admiring expressions from the ladies, who greeted it with a chorus of 'La, la's' and sublime looks of ecstasy, while my soldier friends endeavoured to find relief from its dazzling glory, by many earnest requests to be stricken blind or pink, etc.

Shirts of all colours were handed around to the remainder, who, finding that the ladies evinced no signs of assisting them in the operations of exchange, quickly donned them, and we sat around looking like a harem full of Queens of Sheba.

Our spirits automatically tuned up to these gay habiliments and we became endowed with a fiercely joyous feeling as we lounged about the bright and comfortable fire.

Glasses of scalding hot and delicious coffee were given us by these good people, rendering our comfort complete.

The inhabitants of this town, which to the best of my recollection was called Caudry, proved very solicitous for our comfort and welfare.

This was extraordinary, as they were perfectly well aware that the enemy were close upon our heels and likely to appear at any moment. I imagine that most people could have been far too concerned with their own impending troubles to worry about those of others.

Our hosts of this town, no doubt, remembered their own fathers, sons and brothers who were absent engaged elsewhere in the defence of their country, with many a prayer that they, in their need, would receive such kindly treatment at other hands.

We felt fit to face the world again, at least I did, but for the exception of the condition of my feet.

I had attempted to remove my boots during this rest, but desisted in the attempt on finding that most of the skin had been rubbed away and the resulting bleeding mass had congealed to the boots. I dreaded the moment when I would be called upon to set them working again.

This soon arrived, as, the rain having abated, shrill whistles bade us leave the comfort of the house, and to parade.

With many expressions of gratitude to our Good Samaritans, I hobbled painfully outside.

Walking upon hot bricks could not hold greater agonies than those inflicted by the pangs that seared my feet. That I was not alone in my suffering was evident by the imprecations that arose as the column started off.

On and on we went, until the monotonous rising and falling of our bloated and bleeding nether extremities produced a pain so intense that by a merciful intervention of Providence became more than our suffering nerves could bear and remain conscious of, and they gave up the struggle and subsided into numbness.

Even in these trying moments the irrepressible and unconquerable cockney wag punctuated the air at intervals with cheery comments of great good humour:

'Gor lummy! look at ole Alf practisin' step dancin'! I'll lay 'es workin' up 'is turn for the Ol' 'Olborn. Ain't it a fair treat. 'Op to it, Alf!'

He followed up this sally by whistling 'Pop goes the weasel,' the time being alternately accelerated or retarded according to the speed in which the unfortunate Alf placed his feet upon the road.

'Why don't cher try walkin' on yer 'ands, Bert? and give yer feet a rest; they allus did look so much alike that it can't make no odds. It's a fair knockart to me

'ow yer tells the difference,' furnishes another speci-
men which did much to help us on our way.

We proceeded in this manner through the darkness
of the night, sleeping as we marched, suffering rude
awakenings at intervals at the various halts.

The advent of these were heralded by a series of
crashes, followed by good solid curses, as the rear sections piled into those that had halted in front of them,
notifying them of the stop by the means of painful
collisions, providing a very fair imitation of a heavy
and lumbering goods train executing a similar
manœuvre.

At each halt we all dropped like stones to the ground,
and nursed and massaged our feet, now reduced to
bleeding rags, amidst sonorous curses which came
from the very bottom of the heart.

Some of the men, unable to bear the pain longer, tore
off their red-hot chambers of torture in which their
feet had been imprisoned for so long.

The horrors of war thus revealed were terrible to
contemplate.

After being eased in this manner, they defied all
attempts to get them back into the boots in preparation for the continuation of our progress, and the
men who had unwisely succumbed to this temptation
were forced to protect their feet by binding them
around with the puttees they had removed from
their legs and to carry their boots slung around their
necks.

In the early hours of the next morning, we stopped on
the outskirts of a village.

For some time I had been aware that we could no longer hear the ominous thunder of gunfire, and so gained an erroneous impression that we had outstripped the enemy to such an extent that we would probably be able to obtain a holiday from the War for quite a few days. If such happiness should prove the case I made up my mind, in advance, to spend every minute of it with my feet hung up well off the ground. Contemplation of such a blissful condition formed the entire occupation of my mind, and dreaming of these glorious possibilities I fell asleep. Only for a few seconds and then I was made painfully aware that this heaven had not yet been reached by an order to get up and move on again.

Our great grief was lightened by the wonderful information that we were going into billets, and after slouching into the village we were conducted to a barn.

This was a small building composed of two stories.

We led in, the first of us being directed up a ladder until every inch of the top floor was occupied, with the exception of the hole that gave admittance to it from the floor below.

The ground floor was then similarly covered, and the small overflow of men, who could not be accommodated, were housed in some deserted pig-pens, standing outside the barn. Throwing ourselves upon the hard floor, we engaged in a terrific struggle to secure sufficient room to enable us to stretch our aching limbs.

I hastened to tear off my boots and what remained of my socks, and a blistering sight greeted me.

Two sorry objects strongly resembling bruised and

torn kidneys, were revealed in the place of my erstwhile dainty feet.

While I was gently and tenderly massaging them, I
saw the man next to me groping at the neck of a small
sack.

I had noticed this sack being carried slung on his
back during the march, and it had excited my
curiosity, especially as I thought I could observe movement within it. I had also been slightly puzzled by
mysterious smothered screams, coming from somewhere within my vicinity, which I vainly suspected
originated from that sack, but I had lacked the energy
to ask questions on the subject.

As he now, therefore, showed signs of revealing his
secret unasked, I watched him intently as he gently
manipulated the fastenings. The string removed, he
pulled it gently open, and peered into its depths, making an encouraging sound with his mouth the while.

A great commotion in the interior of the bag answered his efforts, and, to my unbounded amazement,
a small and perky head of a little white pig, a couple
of weeks old, appeared.

Smiling happily, the soldier tenderly drew it forth,
and, sitting it upright, dangled it upon his knee. As
proud as a father with his first-born, he fondled that
little beast, calling it by most absurd terms of endear-
ment that would have caused an elderly spinster's pet
poodle to turn bilious with envy.

This little pig, however, had other ideas, and appeared to be hunting for something which claimed its
attention to the exclusion of all else.

Not being able to discover the object of its frantic search it set up a terrific squealing, that soon brought everybody alert with frightful curses. This almost caused a fight between the owner of the pig and the remainder, until the atom of potential pork, finding by a lucky chance its owner's finger, sucked at that digit voraciously, and immediately became quiet. The man then laid himself down, with the piglet snuggled down on one of his arms, with the finger of his other hand deputising as a mother, to the animal's huge contentment.

This presented a most laughable picture, the man of war lying there crooning and making mother noises to his adopted baby, while the latter rested with great confidence against him, his bright little eyes sparkling with childlike mischief.

I asked him how and where he had obtained it, for I was curious, as he was one of the men that had accompanied me to the farm to get water and incidentally to search for food on the morning of the 24th.

He told me that he had found it hidden in the manger of an empty horse box on that morning, and took it at first with the intention of converting it into food.

The fact that we had been able to obtain the means of staving off our hunger had brought a reprieve to the little mite, which now lay complacently ignorant of the vile and untimely fate which at one time threatened it.

I asked him if he had any intention of killing and eating it later on, in the event of a repetition of the failure of food supplies, and his furious reply:

'Whatcher take me for, a blinkin' cannibal?' both flabbergasted and amused me.

Musing on the strangeness of human nature, I sank into slumber.

A terrible commotion awoke me, and I saw a crowd of men, pale even beneath the grime which almost concealed the features of their faces, gathered around the open trapdoor in the floor of the loft, gazing below with strange looks of horror.

Hastily going to their side, I inquired the reason for this turmoil, and made the depressing discovery that owing to our crowded conditions, a rifle had been accidentally knocked through it, and had fallen, butt first, on to the head of a man sleeping immediately beneath, and had crushed in his head and instantly killed him before he had time to awaken.

I was thus taught that tragedy and humour oft go hand in hand.

Returning miserably to my couch, I once again resumed my tragically interrupted slumbers, in which I remained comfortably immersed until well into the morning of the 26th of August.

o

CHAPTER XIII

THE awakening this morning was quite calm and peaceful after the turmoil of the preceding three days, our much-needed repose having refreshed us wonderfully and to a slight extent soothed our aches and pains.

A cheerful air was assumed, and we discussed gaily a pleasant rumour that some idiot had circulated while we sat around in our billet feeding. The rumour was to the effect that the battalion, having been so decimated (about this time 200 in strength), it had been decided to entrain us, and to dispatch us to a base for refitting and reinforcements, to bring us up to establishment numbers

As prophesied, experience had taught us all we desired to know of war, and equipped with this knowledge, that had been purchased at a heavy price, I hastily revised my previous notions, and mentally apologised to those wise men, who, through their utterance of words of warning and condemnation, I had, at one time considered fools.

My sleeping companion the 'pigman,' sat on his haunches, his little pig perched on his knee, feeding it carefully with army biscuit, laboriously brought to the required moisture and softness by the process of chewing.

As each morsel became ready, he conveyed it on one of his fingers, to the mouth of the pig (which had been unanimously accorded the name of 'Percy') which eagerly awaited its arrival, and devoured it with avidity.

Little 'Percy' proved a hard taskmaster, his insistent demands that his voracious appetite be satisfied permitted his owner small chance of swallowing food for his own nourishment. If a further supply of food was not immediately forthcoming, little 'Percy' showed his resentment in a shrill outburst of high-pitched grunts and squeals, only to be stopped by the application of the food-laden finger.

We all took 'Percy' to our hearts, in spite of his funny little drawbacks, and were all most anxious to keep him with us, and most of us were prepared to increase our affection to the extent of taking him to our stomachs, in the event of certain emergencies arising. Fortunately for his peace of mind dear little 'Percy' did not suspect our hungry love for him.

Any attempt on the part of the remainder of us to pay some little attention to 'Percy' was resentfully rebuffed by his nurse in no uncertain manner. This resulted in him being subjected to a great deal of ragging.

'Ain't 'e like the ole man?' said one.

'What a shime, you carn't blime the poor little blighter fer that,' answered another, and chucking 'Percy' under the chin, he continued hopefully:

'Don't chew tike that ter 'eart, cock! praps yer might grow aht of it!'

All this being met by furious scowls of the 'pigman', naturally it caused us a great deal of uproarious laughter.

At the height of these proceedings we were given an entertainment, entailing a great deal of spirited action on our part, and only really appreciated some little time after the staging of it. With a loud crash something struck the tiles of the roof of our barn, passed through them, and dropped on to the only particle of open space available in that crowded billet.

With eyes emulating those of crabs, we saw that it was a shell of small calibre, and we sat around it, frozen into immobility by the shock, awaiting in awful suspense for it to burst and blow us all to fragments.

I clearly remember the picture we presented. The shell gyrating madly on its own axis, the strained poses of the men as they sat in all manner of positions, some with their hands arrested in mid-air in the act of conveying food to their mouths, their intended journey forgotten.

It certainly looked as though our previous hopes of getting away from the War were about to be realised in a manner, far more rapid and undesirable than we anticipated.

The tension was broken by an abrupt movement made by a man sitting near the open trap-door. He, recovering his wits, with a mighty spring, dived head foremost through the hole on to the floor below.

This action produced in the remainder of us a simultaneous and vigorous activity, as we emulated, and easily outdid the forerunner in the prodigious leaps we made for that hole, and safety.

Such a bunch of us arrived at the orifice at the same moment that we hung jammed together in it, and only obtained the release that enabled us to drop through, and away from the sticky end that threatened us to the floor below, after a frantic struggle, the use of the ladder being spurned as a much too tardy means of exit.

Reaching the floor with a series of plops like the falling of over-ripe fruit, we hastily gathered ourselves up from among the legitimate occupants upon whom we had so unceremoniously fallen, and, without wasting either time or breath on explanations, we dashed out, and continued to run until we had reached a spot of safety, where we turned to observe the flight of our temporary home through the ether.

Whilst waiting for this interesting development, we saw our comrades of the ground floor flat, suddenly burst forth evincing signs of great perturbation and still greater haste.

I guessed that they, exceedingly puzzled by our inexplicable behaviour, had investigated its cause and upon ascertaining it, wasted no time in following the eminently sound example set by us.

We waited in vain for the explosion to take place, and after about twenty minutes, a couple of heroes volunteered to reconnoitre.

They entered the billet, and then re-appeared, rolling all over the place, and roaring with laughter.

We hastened forward to find the cause of this unseemly mirth, but all they were capable of doing in reply to our queries was to point helplessly to the scene of the incident, while tears poured from their eyes.

Gingerly I mounted the ladder, and found the unceremonious invader lying quiescent, docilely serving as a headrest to little 'Percy', who lay sound asleep across it, without a tremor or fear in the world, happy in his blissful ignorance.

Gently removing the menace to a safe distance outside, to the accompaniment of the remonstrative grunts of 'Percy', thus again making it a fit place for 'heroes', we took possession, gathering round and paying humble and respectful homage to the hero of the adventure, who received it quite unconcernedly amid our hilarious laughter.

That this shell, arriving with its force almost spent, was a lone wanderer that had inexplicably lost its way was the explanation accepted generally, with sighs of relief.

I, personally, entertained grave doubts on the subject, which I decided to keep to myself, as no good could come of distributing ideas that would have an adverse effect on our present high spirits. I was rather surprised to find that no further shells did make their appearance, and I began to think that, after all, the explanation arrived at might be sound.

Orders were now issued to us to prepare to move away, and we paraded entertaining fond hopes that our destination was to be a railway station occupied by a train anxious to support the truth of the rumour we had heard by bearing us to a base.

Our suspicions that all was not well were aroused by the issue to us of business-like looking entrenching tools. These certainly didn't fit in with the 'base' theory as we had interpreted the word, but certainly did imply that the use of the word base was well justified in connection with the operations now contemplated.

Following our officers, somewhat disappointed and crestfallen, we were led to ground selected in front of the village, and exhorted to make nice deep trenches.

This village was named 'Audencourt' and it lay almost halfway between Cambrai and Le Cateau, and formed part of that famous line of defence.

We spat resignedly upon our hands and commenced our toil with the best spirit we could command.

After being engaged at this work about a quarter of an hour the first herald of the hate of the enemy arttillery arrived, giving me justification for my opinion regarding the 'lone' shell earlier on.

The shells came with increasing frequency, falling all over the trenches we were striving to create, exacting their toll, and filling us with a frenzy of effort as we strove madly to provide ourselves with cover from the nerve-destroying blasts. We received tremendous encouragement from the conduct of our officers, and by our commanding officer in particular. He moved coolly among us, always to be found where the trouble was fiercest, with his hands in his pockets and pipe in mouth, setting an example of cool courage which we strove mightily to emulate.

Our energy finally bore fruit in an excavation which, although exceedingly poor defence against artillery fire, was at least less exposed to its effects than standing in the open.

The bombardment had become intense, when, above the din, arose a plaintive voice raised in a pitiful appeal.

'Piggy! Piggy! come back 'ere or you'll get 'urt,' seconded by a stentorian chorus urging one, 'Percy', to show good sense and return to his 'father'.

This extra vocal uproar drew my attention to a spot where I perceived poor little 'Percy' rushing to and fro in utmost bewilderment, scared out of his senses by the shells that burst around him, while his owner stood with his arms thrown out entreatingly, tearfully pleading with 'Percy' to induce him to return to the comparative safety of the trench.

Finding that his appeals were unavailing, the owner suddenly sprang out into the open and ran forward to secure his charge from harm.

After a short and exciting skirmish, he succeeded in catching him, and, gathering him up, turned to regain shelter.

Alas! that was poor little 'Percy's swan song, for before the trench was regained a splinter from a shell raked him through, and wrote finis to his young life.

The end of our potential mascot, which had every opportunity of becoming famous, cast gloom over all, and sad glances were bent on its erstwhile owner while he reverently placed the little corpse in the bottom of the trench.

The shelling of our position continued throughout the day, punctuated by lulls of short duration, which were very thankfully received.

The enemy infantry could only be seen by the aid of powerful glasses, and then only spasmodically, as they moved about the position they had taken up about 2,000 yards from our front. They had evidently too much respect for our powers with our rifles to venture until the artillery had blown us away, and enabled them to advance at a cheaper price; consequently we did not have much to occupy our minds except to look after the wounded who, whenever opportunity offered, were taken to the rear.

We had been told, when first occupying this line, that we were to hold on to it, at all costs, until two o'clock in the afternoon. It had now passed four, and still we lingered.

Certain signs were now manifest, however, which conveyed to me the impression that the overdue move was about to be executed.

At this interesting juncture I heard the particular shell, bearing my name upon it, making directly for me, its shrill cry of ecstasy as it spotted me standing out clearly from among the ordinary racket of the others.

With a last joyful shriek, it burst with wild abandon right over me, and I subsided gracefully, paying tribute to its might.

I opened my eyes slowly, and gazed up into a gloriously blue sky, and then wondered suddenly who was being so spiteful as to subject my head to a brutal kicking.

I wearily thrust up my hand to act as a buffer between my sore head and those vicious blows, and then learnt that they were being directed from the inside of my head.

I withdrew my hand and stared at the crimson mess adhering to it uncomprehensively for a moment, and then came remembrance.

I attempted to struggle up, but was forced by an attack of vertigo, to subside.

The shattering explosions of bursting shells had died away, and the air was strangely calm and still.

Again I essayed to rise, this time with more success, and gazed stupidly around.

A dejected, forlorn, khaki-clad figure stood close by me, leaning against the torn side of the trench, his head bowed down and resting on his arms, apparently sobbing bitterly.

Feeling my head gingerly, I mechanically noted that with the exception of dozens of forms lying pathetically still in queer attitudes, and this man, the position was deserted.

I discovered that upon the back of my head was a deep groove running from just below the crown to the base, which was bleeding freely, accompanied by great stabbing pains. This had been done by a splinter of shell which had struck me down from directly above.

I slowly ran my hands over the other parts of my anatomy and was relieved to learn, as far as I could discover, that this constituted my sole injury. I therefore extracted my field dressing and clumsily bandaged it, as well as I could manage.

I then approached the man who appeared to be the only other occupant alive, and who continued to emit what I took to be deep sobs of grief, and leant my hand encouragingly upon his shoulder.

No acknowledgement was vouchsafed, until I had repeated this movement several times, and then finally he raised his head, presenting a face ghastly in its paleness and painful expression, and sobbed out a desire to know what I required.

It did not take me long to learn that he was not sobbing of grief, but for breath, having been struck in the lungs.

He gaspingly informed me that he had shared that shell with me, which came just as the battalion retired. He had collapsed for a moment, and the others, obviously believing both him and I dead, had left us where we lay. I now groped my way along the trench and inspected the other occupants, and the fact that I did not find another living survivor confirmed my impression that the wounded had been carried away.

Returning to the badly stricken one I tried to soothe his pain, but my efforts were hopeless.

I remembered that a church a little to our rear had been converted into a dressing post, and with a faint hope that the doctor in charge and his staff would still be found there, I assisted my companion from the trench, and directed his faltering footsteps towards this place.

Great was my joy and relief to find that it had not been abandoned.

We stepped inside and glanced around. Every inch of available space was occupied by badly wounded men, who lay on heaps of straw, which had been provided to make them as comfortable as the circumstances would permit.

Busily engaged among the victims of the attack was a young officer of the Royal Army Medical Corps. Surrounded by the paraphernalia of his profession, coat removed and shirt sleeves rolled up, he swiftly, with an air of efficiency, went about his work, assisted by one medical orderly.

On our appearance, this orderly came over to us and examined my companion gravely. He turned away, reappearing almost immediately with a bundle of straw, which he spread on the porch and, with my assistance, the new patient was lowered on to this improvised bed.

The doctor was advised of this serious additional casualty, and immediately he came over and subjected him to a thorough examination. In the meantime, the orderly cleansed the wound in my head, and applied suitable dressings which afforded me huge relief.

Standing at the entrance of the porch, I took stock of my surroundings.

The church had been struck several times by shells, and this, in spite of the fact that a huge Red Cross flag had been prominently displayed. It still hung fluttering bravely, although half the steeple to which it was affixed had been ruthlessly blown away.

Looking out over the direction of our old position, a movement in the distance caught my eye, and I saw hordes of enemy infantry, about three quarters of a mile away, advancing in the direction of the village.

Feverishly, I rushed into the improvised hospital and warned the doctor of this development. Without pausing for a moment from his work he said:

'That does not concern me in the least, my work is here with these men. As they cannot get away the same applies to me. Don't worry about me, I shall be quite all right.'

'Then I shall try and get clear, sir!' I said. To which he replied.

'Go by all means, you can do nothing here. Good luck.'

Hurrying outside, taking advantage of all cover, I made tracks in the opposite direction to this approaching wave.

I went on unmolested for about a mile, until I came to a cutting. Here a doleful sight presented itself to my gaze, and arrested my progress.

The centre of the picture was held by the ruins of four guns of our Royal Field Artillery. They had caught the effects of the avalanche fully, being completely shattered, while the mutilated bodies of their faithful servants lay around, mute evidence that they had nobly executed their duty.

Two men of this battery appeared to be the sole survivors. One sat on a smashed gun trail, his head bowed into his hands, moaning softly, while his comrade busied himself by collecting the identity discs of his late colleagues.

Other signs of life in the cutting were provided by three privates of my own regiment, one driver of the Army Service Corps, whose wagon had been blown practically from under him, one private of the Royal Scots and one of the Royal Irish Regiment.

I threw myself down among these men and gloomily watched the gunner complete the sad work he had engaged himself in.

We presently all joined in an exchange of mutual conversation, until I suddenly remembered that the clouds of Germans I had seen a short time before were likely to be upon us at any moment.

I rapidly communicated my fears to the others, and I climbed to the edge of the cutting to ascertain the amount of the enemy progress. I was mortified to find that they were a scant three hundred yards distance, and sliding down to my new companions without ceremony, I imparted to them the disturbing knowledge I had gleaned by my brief view.

With one accord we hotfooted it away.

We rushed along under the cover of a bank, until, arriving at the end, we found a small wood and dived into its shelter just as the advanced German troops defiled into the cutting we had so recently and timely evacuated.

They saw us and opened fire, to which we replied with a defiant burst, before turning and scrambling, hell for leather, into the deepest part of that wood, and we continued going until exhaustion bade us stop.

We now held an impromptu conference to discuss our unenvious and perilous situation. They all looked to me, as the senior ranking member of the party, to decide upon our future course of action.

I was sorely exercised as to the best procedure to adopt, having no maps or any idea of the lay of the country, and only a very vague notion of the general direction of the retirement of our army. I decided that our best chance of getting away and keeping away, was to lay a straight course as near as possible as the crow flies, in a direct line away from the direction of the enemy's advance, taking all obstacles in our stride.

I submitted this resolution to the others, who gave it their entire approval, and having all expressed a determination to do everything in our power to resist and avoid capture, we commenced what was to prove a most unusual and interesting adventure.

I was filled with pride at the brave command that had been vested in me, and felt like the whole of the Napoleons rolled into one.

Was I not the commander of a force composed of not only of three different regiments, but also artillery, and a supply column as represented by our friend of the Army Service Corps.

My thoughts were pleasantly interrupted by a 'Faith giniril, 'tis a whowl brigade your havin' here,' the disturber being our Irish friend.

'Aye! a Phantom Brigade' contributed the Scot.

This last remark possessed a flavour pleasantly savouring of the mysterious, and so tickled everybody that we there and then elected unto ourselves this nomenclature, which made us all feel important and jolly.

Crossing fields and fences, hills and dales, we passed leisurely on our way at first, with many an anxious glance towards our rear, but gradually abandoning this watchfulness as we proceeded without interference.

Occasionally we would stumble upon a building, which we would subject to a minute search in the hope of finding something to satisfy our hunger, for we were all pretty well starving, and depended entirely on the country for our sustenance.

We, up to this time, met with no success in this line, as all the houses we struck had been abandoned and emptied of their contents.

Darkness falling, found us still blithely toiling along without interruption, except a slight incident which, at the time threatened to deprive us of our 'commissariat department.'

We were negotiating a large field in the complete darkness, spread out in line, when we were startled by the sounds of a loud splash and a despairing yell, followed by a terrible commotion and an awe inspiring smell coming from the left of our line.

Rushing to the scene of the disturbance, we discovered the whole of our Army Service Corps floundering about in a slimy pool. With encouraging exhortations and advice to save the women and children first, the supply column was rescued from the watery and decidedly unpleasant grave into which he had unfortunately fallen.

Stationing him well to windward, we continued our advance, until, on coming out of the field, we struck a road upon which stood a promising-looking building.

On examination, this proved to be a deserted estaminet which we entered silently with about the same

P

expectations of discovering anything useful to us, in view of our former experiences, as a burglar would entertain on breaking open a gas-meter in Aberdeen.

We spread ourselves all over it, and commenced a thorough examination by the light of matches. Our first discovery was half a dozen half-consumed candles, which we found in the kitchen. Lighting these, we prosecuted our hunt for food. Some bread was next unearthed, which, judging from its condition, had been baked in prehistoric days, and had been preserved as a family heirloom.

A whoop of joy and triumph drew us back into the room that would normally have served as the bar.

Here we found a couple of the boys dancing around a barrel half filled with French beer that they had found under the counter. Without wasting any time we tapped that barrel and were just enjoying our third or fourth taster when we were almost scared stiff by the sounds of riot proceeding from some point outside the building.

Terrified cacklings, mixing with the sounds of falling and scrambling bodies, punctuated by hoarse and excited shouts of encouragement and finally victory, rent the still night air.

Two boisterous, dishevelled-looking apparitions, bursting into the room bearing the corpses of a couple of hens, amply explained the cause of this unseemly commotion.

They had directed their energies to the exploration of the outbuildings, and had surprised and captured these wretched birds.

Possessed of the material promise of a good feast, we decided to remain in the estaminet and do the thing handsomely.

Carefully screening the windows, we built a fire, and procured a couple of saucepans, into which we popped the birds and the stale bread.

We then sat around the fire as happy as sandboys, quaffing flagons of ale, and eyeing with eager anticipation the simmering pots, while waiting for the fowl to cook.

Hardships, suffering and danger were totally forgotten, and we lived only for the present as we gathered around, exchanging good humoured banter, telling yarns, and occasionally breaking into song. We even became so foolish as to venture the opinion that War was not so bad after all.

One of the artillerymen created a humorous diversion by appearing from a cellar-like chamber wearing an old apron he had found, and a huge beard and moustache constructed from the stuffing of an old armchair.

Dangling a napkin over his arm he displayed proudly a bottle, three parts full of cognac, that he had unearthed, and assumed the airs and duties of a 'fully licensed man'.

The food being voted cooked and ready for consumption (this opinion being arrived at mainly because the water was boiling), we drew around a table to enjoy the banquet.

What a fine sight for starving men. We gloated over a table containing unlimited supplies of beer, some cognac, two chickens and plenty of 'soup'.

The birds having been rudely severed into nine more
or less equal portions, they were handed around, and
the only sounds heard for the next few minutes was
the vigorous champing of jaws.

I had always laboured under the impression that
'spring chickens' were of the tenderest variety, but
judging by the effort I found it necessary to make to
dispose of those chicks, I formed the conclusion that,
in their case, the spring part of the business had been
so overdone that it had left no space available for the
chicken. However, our determined onslaughts did
eventually overcome them, and now, being replete, I
suggested a little exercise in aid of our digestion.

Securing every receptacle capable of holding liquid,
and filling them with the precious beer, the erstwhile
publican regretfully resigned his self-imposed duties,
and we went forth into the night, leaving the estaminet
behind us, only because we recognised the impossibility
of taking it along with us.

On becoming accustomed to the gloom, we oriented
ourselves with regard to our direction, and continued
our pilgrimage without anything happening to mar
our pleasant reminiscenses, until just after midnight.

At this time we were jogging along almost half asleep
when we were scared into alertness by the unmistakable sounds of a body of armed men marching across
the front of the direction in which we were proceeding.
We were then moving along on the outskirts of a forest,
and, on hearing these alarming sounds, threw ourselves flat as noiselessly as possible. Shortly afterwards
a body of about two hundred enemy infantry passed

before us, emerging unexpectedly from the forest, along a road that cut clear through it. They passed within fifty yards of the spot wherein we lay with bated breath, and passed out of sight.

I began to fear that we would be compelled to pay for the little indulgence we had permitted ourselves at the house behind us, with the loss of our liberty, or worse.

The scare given us by the unexpected appearance of this body of the enemy, caused us to press on with greater vigour, and with additional precautions against surprises of this nature.

Dawn found us flitting like shadows through this same forest. One man out on each flank and another leading about twenty yards ahead, while the remainder of us followed him in single file.

I trudged along, wondering what fate this new day, the 27th August, held in store for us.

Mercifully the veil was drawn close, but was even at this moment on the verge of being lifted, to disclose the first of a series of shocks and surprises of a nature both pleasant and the reverse.

CHAPTER XIV

THE leading man, reaching the side of a road passing through the forest across the line of our direction, signalled to us to halt while he scanned the road to ascertain if it was clear. Apparently satisfied that it was, he was about to emerge from cover when we saw him start at something that had impinged on his vision, and that froze him into immobility for a moment. Turning swiftly, he came towards us with a rush, and told us that there were a body of men, mounted on cycles, coming along the road in our direction.

We all crept forward and carefully scrutinised these cyclists, and soon acquired the knowledge that they were no friends of ours.

One man rode ahead, and about fifty yards in rear followed ten others, and, as far as we could tell, they were entirely unsupported by other enemy troops.

We hastily conferred together, weighing the pros and cons of the policy of aggression against that of allowing sleeping dogs to lie. Decision was brought to our divided councils by a remark made by one of the artillery section.

He stated emphatically that, as far as he was concerned, he would as lief die as to continue to live amid the agony he was enduring from his feet, which were protesting mightily against the unusual abuse put upon them by all this marching.

The idea of continuing our travels mounted on bicycles was certainly an attractive one, so without more ado, we selected positions for our intended ambuscade of the enemy.

We had the advantage of surprise in delivering our attack, which amply outweighed the enemy's slight superiority in numbers.

We decided that it was necessary to let the leading man pass us unmolested, and we waited, lying in the thick underbrush that grew within a few yards of the side of the road, with palpitating hearts and stifled breath, and fingers itchingly playing with the triggers of our ready rifles, for the arrival of the fateful moment that would decide the issue.

Only a moment, a moment that seemed a period of hours, could have passed, when a creaking announced the advent of cyclist number one.

With tingling apprehension we observed him cast a glance on and over our place of concealment, but, happily for us, entirely unsuspicious of our presence, he continued forging ahead.

The main body appeared immediately after, shouting carefree remarks to one another with the accompaniment of much laughter.

With a hideous crash we slipped into action, rudely curtailing their badinage and jokes, and causing the entire force to collapse, a tangled mass of machines and men, on to the road.

For an instant the pile stilled, and then heaved convulsively again, as six survivors of that volley, most of them wounded, crawled to the opposite side of the road, and valiantly returned our fire.

Their efforts availed them nothing, for we had them at an overwhelming disadvantage, being so well concealed that they could only hazard a guess at our position from the sound of our rifle fire, while they lay fully exposed to us.

A scant few minutes, then the arm of the sole survivor shot up in token of surrender.

We immediately concentrated our attention to our flank, where the first cyclist was busy trying to rake us from that direction. On the outbreak of the firing he had gallantly returned to the scene of action to render all possible aid to his comrades. Seeing the annihilation of his troop, and realising that to continue his resistance was useless, he quickly followed the example set by his compatriot and surrendered.

We carefully left our positions and approached the unfortunate victims, making a careful and comprehensive survey of the road in each direction, without seeing anything to cause us undue alarm.

We gathered together our prisoners, fastened them together with straps taken from their equipment, and sat them back to back in the ditch beside the road.

We then attentively examined the fruits of our victory, which we had gained without suffering a scratch, so complete had been our surprise.

The bicycles were efficient-looking machines, heavy and strongly made, and we each selected one with the exception of our Irishman, who we discovered, to our consternation, did not know how to ride.

However, each cycle was equipped with a serviceable-looking carrier behind, and we decided to take turns in giving him a lift, and in this manner solved this unexpected difficulty.

All being ready, I gave the order to mount and away, as it obviously would have been an exhibition of extremely bad tactics to have remained longer than necessary in the quarter in which we had so well advertised our presence.

We started off, taking the same direction in which the German patrol was travelling before our interruption, and I became considerably concerned by a worrying little question that cropped up: 'Were they going or coming?'

No satisfactory answer seemed forthcoming to the anxious query, and I began to weigh the possibilities that the possession of the bicycles would do us more harm than service, and had almost made up my mind to discard them, and to proceed along our original line on foot, when my anxiety was relieved by the discovery of an intersecting road that led away at right angles, in the very direction I deemed it advisable to pursue.

We changed our course and took this turning, and could see that the road led as straight as a ruled line through the forest, until, at a distance of about half a mile away, it emerged into open country beyond. We pedalled hastily down this avenue, casting fearful glances into the forest looming forbiddingly on either side of us, as we proceeded, expecting momentarily to hear from their depths the peal of fire which would, in turn, end our misguided careers.

On reaching the end of the road unscathed, an occurrence that evoked our hearty expressions of mutual congratulation, we halted, and before exposing ourselves in the open, made a close and careful reconnaisance of the country for signs of the foe.

Finding the beauty of the landscape unmarred by any such nasty sights, we remounted and continued to sail easily along.

This mode of progression certainly had 'footslogging' beaten to nowhere, ensuring a nice, speedy, comfortable means of travel, and we felicitated each other upon the sound commonsense displayed in engaging in the action that had been the means of securing these iron steeds to us.

Moving quickly and happily, we reached the summit of a hill, and finding that from this eminence we commanded a clear view of the surrounding country for at least a mile in every direction, we again subjected every inch to a very careful scrutiny, with a negative result that gave us much satisfaction.

Freed from any danger of sudden surprise and attack, I decided to call a halt for a much-needed rest. This decision was greeted with the utmost enthusiasm.

We now found leisure to devote more attention to our captures.

Each one had a bulky leather satchel strapped to the crossbar of the frame, which we removed and sat down to examine.

I opened mine and looked in, and the contents projected into my vision by this action caused me to gasp in amazed surprise, for it was almost filled with articles of silver.

Delving into the bag, I removed dozens of solid silver knives, forks and spoons, and also two beautifully-chased silver mugs, but the things that really appealed to me more than any other I found at the very bottom.

A bottle of wine, a large hunk of bread, some butter, and a tin of potted meat.

The air was full of exclamations of wonder, as the others pawed over the articles found in the bags that had fallen to their lot. Watches, bracelets, and silverware of every description, lay strewn all over the grass where we sat. Those Huns had collected the entire contents of some unfortunate silversmith's shop.

As my companions caught sight of the real treasures yielded by my bag they promptly forgot the silverware, and concentrated on the interior of their bags in a frenzied hope of making a discovery of equal importance to mine in the form of food, with great success, to everybody's comfort.

We regaled ourselves upon this abundance of good food and drink, until we had sated our appetites, and, after drawing lots to select a sentry, we settled down to enjoy an hour's nap.

We were awakened by our look-out at the end of the hour, and, with the country still bathed in tranquillity, we hopped on to our steeds and pushed away along the trail that would, we fondly hoped, eventually lead us to safety.

The fact that we had not caught up to our own army perturbed me mightily, for we had been travelling constantly for the last twenty-four hours with scarcely a stop, and we must have covered, with the aid of both our bicycles and our feet, between twenty-five to thirty miles of ground.

I could not understand this phenomenon at the time, but was considerably amused, and more or less amazed, at our extraordinary good fortune in evading capture, on learning later the reason for our failure to make contact.

We had marched on a line that proceeded diagonally so faithfully that it had kept us the whole time midway between our retreating army and the advancing German forces.

We had covered about five miles since last halting, and were half-way up the slope of a small hill, when we were surprised by the thunderous sounds of charging horses' feet coming behind us.

A glance around filled us with consternation, as we beheld a band of at least thirty Uhlans charging down, with wild whoops, upon us.

We leapt from our machines, and sprang for the only possible positions of temporary safety, automatically.

This was the top of a bank about ten feet high that bounded the road upon one side at this point. They came so near getting us that my rifle was, for a moment, imprisoned, as the point of a lance went between the sling and the barrel, pinning it to the side of the incline as I drew myself clear over the top of the embankment.

Dashing past us, impelled by the momentum of their vicious onslaught, they presented to us the splendid target of their backs, an opportunity of which we took such good advantage that their ardour became suddenly checked.

Dismounting from their chargers, they proceeded to continue their attack upon us on foot, some of them climbing out on the bank higher up above us, and subjecting us to a worrying fire, whilst others engaged us from the road below.

We soon learnt, with great dismay, that another portion of this enemy party had worked down the road and had mounted the bank below us, and had opened a harassing fire upon us.

We were, by these tactics, practically surrounded, and any attempt at escape rendered impossible.

We had been extremely lucky so far, but we all entertained the feeling that such good fortune could not possibly last, and was bound to end some time. Now it had arrived, for we had not an earthly chance against the odds facing us.

Grimly we fought on in desperation, expecting every moment to see the end of the farce.

Four of our party were struck, fortunately not seriously enough to place them *hors de combat*, and we started to bid each other a fond farewell.

At my side, which was near the edge of the top of the bank, I became aware of a scrambling, and turned to see the heads of half a dozen of the enemy mounting over the top. Shouting for assistance, I desperately engaged this new menace with the bayonet. Three or four others sprang to my succour, and we madly stabbed and thrust in an effort to keep our fate at bay.

When all hope had fled, more sounds of charging horses became audible above the clash of arms, and with a mad cheer a troop of British cavalry swept into view, scattering our attackers like chaff.

Nearly fainting with exhaustion and excitement, we did our best to assist our rescuers in their task of subjugating the enemy, with such success that he was put to flight, leaving us victorious on the field.

Our cavalrymen returning with seven unwounded prisoners, we hastened to pay our respects and gratitude for their timely deliverance of us from our very awkward predicament.

Our saviours were a lancer patrol consisting of twenty odd men under the command of a sergeant.

We examined the battlefield, on which we found lying six enemy dead and eight wounded.

The sergeant imparted to us the good news that we were quite close to our own army, which lay on a course at right angles to the one we had been pursuing.

It was then that I learnt that we had been travelling parallel between the two armies.

Receiving concise directions as to the route to be followed to reach our objective, we left the troop, happy, and relieved in the knowledge that we were in contact with our forces at last, and with a prayer of thanksgiving for the successful issue from the attempt the enemy had made to nip our gay careers in the bud.

We repaired to our bicycles, and on rescuing them from the spot on which they had been hurriedly

thrown, we found that they had all, more or less, suffered damage by being trampled upon. This ill usage
had put three of them out of commission.

We managed quite well, and, carefully following
the instructions we had received to guide us on our
route, we careered along, four of the machines being
doubly burdened, until our progress was arrested by
a river.

The bridge that had once afforded the means of
crossing had been blown clean away. We could not
gauge the depth of the river, so our Army Service
Corps detail volunteered to strip and try it out. He was
very fond of water, that chap.

Undressing, he dived in, and we soon learnt that, at
its deepest, it was no more than five feet.

With one accord, on acquiring this information, we
followed his example and stripped.

First we gathered our clothing into bundles, and,
holding them well out of the water upon our heads,
ferried them across to the other side. Returning, we
performed like offices for our arms, equipment and
bicycles.

The feel of water, after being strangers to it so long,
was glorious, and as soon as we had moved everything
over, we could not resist the temptation to turn back
and revel in the refreshing caress of that river.

We dived and splashed and romped about, and enjoyed ourselves like a lot of kids, entirely without care
or thought of danger.

Utilising a rolled up puttee as a ball, we indulged in a
strenuous game of water polo for some time.

Eventually, tiring of this sport, we scrambled out and resumed our clothing.

The bandage about my head had now come off, and I was amazed at the rapid rate of progress toward recovery the wound was making. With the assistance of one of my comrades it was rebound, and we all carried on up the hill running from the river, until we arrived at the crest, about three hundred yards distance from the scene of our aquatic exploits.

Arriving at this eyrie, we glanced out over the farther side where we saw the welcome spectacle of the British Army apparently very busy preparing positions of defence five or six hundred yards away.

Now that we were well within sight of our long-sought goal, we decided that there was no immediate need to join them, for it would be far better to remain where we were until they had finished digging, so that there would be no danger of us running into that kind of thing.

Service in a free lance army was much more acceptable than the other, we unanimously agreed; and we decided that, as we were now perfectly secure, we would preserve our independence a while longer, and rest where we were.

There we lay, like storm-battered sea-dogs resting in the calm and safety of the harbour.

We freely discussed the war in all the phases we had experienced, and concluded that although there were occasional bright spots, they were few and far between, and the horrors rendered the very small amount of

Q

glory very insignificant by comparison. As one of the London lads put it:

'The blokes what makes such a shout about the glory to be found in war must have got their ideas in the Salvation Army.'

One of our number, foraging about, now captured a hedgehog, which he brought back to the circle with him. Here, with a very businesslike air, he produced his knife and killed it.

I was rather surprised at this brutal and wanton action, and I asked him why he had done it.

'Ter eat o' course,' he replied, smacking his lips and evincing signs of anticipation of gastronomic pleasure.

The body of the little beast was enclosed in a ball of clay. A fire was kindled and the ball placed in it and covered over. The remainder sat around watching these proceedings with great interest, not unmixed with repulsion at the thought of anybody eating such a thing.

Presently, the ball having cracked open through the effects of the heat, our gourmet removed it, and, breaking it in half, exposed to our view the steaming carcase of the hedgehog, devoid of all its bristles, which had been left imprisoned in the clay.

The result was a tasty-looking and pleasant smelling morsel.

He handed this product of his culinary prowess around, permitting each of us to take one small pinch by way of a taster, and, as he put it, to teach us to refrain from sneering at the knowledge possessed by our betters.

It proved extremely succulent and delicious, and we sat around him, enviously watching him with watering mouths, like a crowd of expectant hounds, as he consumed the remainder with aggravating noises of profound enjoyment and satisfaction.

A startled tirade by our Irishman jerked us out of the state of somnolence into which we had drifted.

'Be the holy saints, the blackguards we've just been after killin' are not dead at all, for there comes ivery wan uv them.' Following the direction of his outstretched finger, we saw, with great concern, numerous bodies of enemy infantry approaching the river from the other side.

We had foolishly imagined them to be many miles away, and now here they were again almost on top of us. That supplied the reason for the vigorous defensive preparations being executed by the British troops in our rear; they were expecting these visitors if we were not.

We remembered that we had the unbridged river between us, so we decided to stay awhile and keep observation upon them for as long as possible. Our rear was quite clear, and on our bicycles, on the good road running downhill to the positions behind us we could rapidly cover the distance intervening between us and safety.

We therefore proceeded to view the movements of these troops with the greatest interest.

Snuggled down out of sight, closely, we saw the vanguard of the enemy reach the side of the river, where they prowled restlessly up and down, obviously looking for some means by which they could cross, throwing glances, fraught with apprehension, in our general direction, although I am certain they were not aware of our nearness.

Finding that no bridges existed in the immediate neighbourhood, they apparently decided to cross in the same manner previously adopted by us. They reluctantly stripped themselves of their clothing, stepped gingerly into the river, and, holding their coverings above their heads, commenced to wade across.

We lay watching this manœuvre with glistening eyes, rooted to the spot by fascination.

Quite a crowd of German troops had by this time assembled on the opposite bank, and on seeing their advance guard arrive safely across, they commenced to hastily undress and follow suit.

Soon both banks were covered by men in all stages of undress, those on the side nearest us in the process of dressing and those on the other side busy disrobing, while the river swarmed with naked men wading slowly across.

This opportunity was too good to miss, and proved fatal to our resolutions, based on sound common sense to lay low and say nothing.

I glanced at the other lads and found them all wearing expressions that undoubtedly pleaded for immediate action, and so I rapped out 'Let 'em have it!' And we did, putting all our finest workmanship into the burst of rapid fire that we poured into that mob, instilling them with indescribable fear and panic.

Those left standing on our side of the river plunged, just as they were, back into the stream. The men on the other side attempted a retreat, presenting a spectacle that filled our eyes with the tears of laughter. Some floundered helplessly and comically as their trousers, hanging down around their ankles, tripped them as they ran. Others, wearing but their shirts, ran with the tails of these garments streaming out behind them fluttering in the strong breeze created by the speed of their going. Yet others pranced about naked as the day on which they were born.

We gurgled and choked with laughter, as we sprayed their bare hides with lead, only ceasing to pour out our deadly hail sufficiently long enough to enable us to clear our eyes of the tears that were blinding them.

Fully clothed reinforcements appeared and engaged us viciously in an attempt to wipe out the indignity that had been inflicted upon the Kaiser's soldiers.

Possessed of the slightest atom of sense, I would have ordered a retirement at this juncture, but, being over-ruled by the influence of a pervading spirit of invincibility, I chose to continue the action, being strengthened in this resolve by the sight of lines of our troops advancing from the positions in rear towards the scene, attracted by the sounds of our engagement.

Passing the word along to await the arrival of these troops, we cheerfully continued our defiance.

I was thrusting a clip of cartridges into the chamber of my rifle when suddenly, for some unaccountable reason, the arm performing this operation attempted to fly away from me. Jerking it back to ascertain the cause, I discovered that a stream of blood was spurting gaily from either side of my right wrist, where it had been shot clean through by a bullet.

Three of the others received slight wounds at about the same instant, and I strongly suspected that it was the work of a machine gun, I therefore issued an order to slip back a bit and take advantage of the cover to be found a little lower down the ridge.

I foolishly stood up to retreat, and had not gone two paces before I was again struck, in the right heel. Almost at the same moment I heard my second exclusive visitor from the 'Boche' artillery winging its airy way towards me. I heard its progress right up to the moment that it seemed to poise gracefully above me and burst. Several tons seemed to fall on my right shoulder and thrust me clean through the ground.

I returned to consciousness with a feeling that the whole of my right side had been torn away and replaced by a painful and aching void.

I felt slowly about me and found that on the top of my right shoulder existed a torn and gaping hole, while every attempt to draw breath was accompanied by agony untold, and blood frothingly oozed from my mouth and nostrils.

I guessed that this was the end, for I knew that in addition to the other minor injuries inflicted, they had got me in the lungs.

It was now quite dark, and I could see nothing, but my ears caught the sound of retreating troops, which I knew to be British, as I caught scraps of their con-

versation. They were evidently the troops I had seen
coming up to us from the position behind.

I essayed a shout which only resulted in a frothy
burbling and a nerve-tearing pain in my chest.

I fell to musing on the fate of my late merry command
of the 'Phantom Brigade', none of whom I have ever
seen again to this day, and in conning over our foolishness in neglecting to move to safety when the occasion
offered.

An absurd ballad of sentimental rubbish persisted
in claiming the attention of my thoughts. I had
often heard it produced in the canteen by drunken
soldiers in the last stage of maudlin sentimentality,
and now its cheerful refrain kept running through
my head

> ' Just tike the news to muvver
> An' tell 'er that I luv 'er
> Tell 'er not ter wite fer me
> For I'm not a'comin' 'ome.'

Finally, driven in desperation by the uninspiring
pictures conjured up by this imaginary dirge to frenzied endeavours, I decided that if I was to die it would
be far more desirable if that interesting little event
should happen whilst I was keeping my mind actively
employed on an attempt to reach the main body.
There certainly was no sense lying there alone with
my morbid thoughts.

Transforming my resolution into action, I started off
with set teeth, painfully dragging my agonised body
over the rough and pitiless ground.

I seemed to crawl in this manner for ages, every move
a damnable torture, slipping often into unconsciousness through exhaustion and loss of blood and the
excruciating agony caused by the movements.

Eventually, as the grey light of the 28th August was
paling the sky, I arrived, crawling on my hands and
knees which were now hanging ribands, within hailing
distance of the objective towards which I had struggled
so painfully through the night.

In my anxiety I attempted to draw the attention of
the defenders of the position to my presence and plight
by delivering a mighty shout. This effort proved too
much for my torn lung to stand, and caused me so
much agony that I swooned.

CHAPTER XV

I OPENED my eyes and stared into the heavens, and lay wondering dully at the pains that gnawed at me in every part of my body, and at the awful noise raging in my vicinity.

Gradually recovering, I began to remember the events of the night before, and eventually traced them up to the time I had collapsed at the very threshold of my desire.

I tried several times to rise, but was forced to desist, to relieve the agony in my stiffened wounds.

Finally, however, by a stupendous and agonising effort, I was at last able to draw myself up sufficiently to permit me to glance about.

Behind me on the hill that had witnessed me receive my *congé* the enemy infantry were in force. I could not observe any signs of activity on the part of the occupants of the British position on my immediate front, about which shells were still falling spasmodically, and I was afraid to shout because of the intense suffering it had inflicted upon me in my previous attempt.

Struggling frantically, I wriggled my way forward towards this position, until I finally tumbled over the edge on to some corpses lying in the bottom of the trench.

I had recovered consciousness just a few minutes too late to obtain any succour and relief, as it was obvious that this position had been very recently evacuated, and I saw British troops disappearing in the distance at the other side of a small hamlet that stood about three hundred yards in the rear.

Dispirited, I almost surrendered myself to the inevitable, but happening to glance along towards my flank, I was considerably encouraged to see one of our guns a short distance away on the other side of a road, that ran back into a hamlet, very much in action, being served by four or five men.

I gave a last look around the trench I was in, which was for the greater part, obliterated, and contained a great number of its original bold defenders, now for ever rendered helpless.

The troops that had been holding this position had suffered enormously.

I heaved myself out of that trench and crawled along towards the hamlet, hugging a shallow ditch that ran alongside the road.

Still the lone gun on my right was being frantically worked by those British artillerymen, sending out a shower of shells towards the enemy with a fine show and spirit of unconquerable defiance.

I reached the hamlet, which was deserted, and crawled through it; shells were dropping about it, which filled me now with terror, as I could only progress at a snail's pace on my lacerated hands and knees.

I managed to work through the hamlet, and arriving out at the opposite side, I found myself confronted by three branching roads. As I knelt there, trying to make up my mind which one to follow, the sun went out, and I passed away for the third time, outraged nature's protest against the awful abuse she was being subjected to.

My next awakening was distinctly rude. I became semi-conscious, and lay with my eyes closed, a prey to the most serious misgivings. My body felt as though it was being kicked, and stabbed all over.

It suddenly flashed upon me that I was lying surrounded by Germans, who were fiendishly kicking and bayoneting my poor wrecked body.

'You filthy, bloody swine,' I muttered, 'stop throwing me about, and end it.'

'Hullo! me dear, so you'me not dead then, no not be long chalks to my way o' thinking.'

Like music from heaven that West County dialect penetrated my sorely bemused senses, and brought my eyes open with a snap.

I gazed up into a pair of steady eyes, twinkling with humour, and encouragement, set in a rugged, homely face, a face that perhaps only a mother would be proud of, but to me by far the sweetest face I'd e'er gazed on, surmounted by a khaki cap bearing a badge that has since held a prominent place in my affections.

Clasped safely in the arms of this benevolent giant, I was being borne along on the limber of a field gun. Hence the sensations of being tossed about, and pain that had assailed me on my return to consciousness.

This proved to be the very gun that had excited my admiration by its devotion to duty at the hamlet outside which I had experienced my last collapse.

My new found Samaritan helped me into an upright position, and, as I clung to the wildly swaying vehicle, attempted to wash my wounds, using the contents of his water-bottle, and then to bandage them. He succeeded after a fashion, which brought me a great deal of relief.

He then imparted to me the story of my rescue.

The gun, manned by a sergeant and four men, had been in action since daybreak that morning, and they had all sworn to stick where they were until their last shell had been exhausted. In their great endeavour they had been on the verge of capture, or destruction, and the last shots were fired at point blank range into the ranks of the enemy infantry as they closed upon their prey, creating frightful havoc among them.

Their oath fulfilled, with their last shell gone, in the very face of the enemy they limbered up their gun, and galloped furiously away.

Dashing through the village exposed to a perfect tornado of shot, the leading driver had discovered my bleeding and unconscious form lying across and blocking the road. Finding that it would be impossible to pass without riding over me, he, not being able to bear the thought of committing, to his mind, such an irreverent act, although fully convinced that I was dead, pulled up his horses, and shouted out a request for somebody to move me out of the way.

My gunner friend had jumped off the limber, and approached me to comply with this request. He discovered, to his surprise when he lifted me to place me clear, that I was alive. He thereupon bore me in his arms to the gun, and away we all continued, the whole of this incident occurring amid a terrific fire that was being directed upon them by the mortified enemy.

In time we caught up with our troops, and passed through their line.

Immediately we had attained this temporary security, the horses were slowed down to a walk, for which I was extremely grateful, as it relieved my aches and pains enormously, and assisted my wounds to stop bleeding.

We jogged along, the sergeant making frequent inquiries in the hope of ascertaining the whereabouts of the division to which he was attached, and of securing further supplies of ammunition.

Eventually a motor ambulance came along and my rescuers hailed it, I transferred myself to it from the gun that had been my haven of refuge, and with deep and grateful thanks, I bade these gallant artillerymen farewell.

In the ambulance was an orderly of the Royal Army Medical Corps, who immediately busied himself by giving my wounds some much-needed professional attention. When this was done I was given some beef tea, and, lying more comfortably than I had dreamed would be possible a few hours before, I gave up the dying idea and surrendered myself to sleep.

This was first broken when I was transferred to a train of cattle trucks, fully occupied by hundreds of wounded, who were lying about the bare floor of the wagons.

Every time that train stopped, or started, we were subjected to a hellish torture, as each truck bumped or crushed into another, causing the air to resound with frightful cries of agony from the poor devils most badly wounded.

We, in our wretched train, arrived at Rouen, and were taken into a temporary hospital, and put immediately to bed, of which I took the fullest advantage by straightway relapsing into slumber, for I had a terrible amount of leeway to pull up in that line.

I next awoke, roused by a voice asking if I would like to go to England, to see a cheerful smiling doctor standing at the foot of my cot. He directed an orderly to hand me my clothes, and I sprung out of bed with the intention of getting into them, and fell prone and unconscious on to my face.

I next recovered to a gentle swaying movement, that puzzled me greatly for a moment, until I saw a sailor busy doing a kindly act with a bucket and a mop.

We arrived at Southampton, and as I lay on a stretcher on the quayside, crowds thronged around in admiration and pity.

I wanted neither of these, I wanted a good cigarette, and presently I was showered with them. I took one and nearly died, for I had forgotten my lung. My smoking days were over for some time to come.

Later on, when in a train, I had the curiosity to ask somebody whither we were bound, and to my delight he answered—Plymouth.

Arriving at Plymouth on September 3rd, 1914, I had thus seen the world, both heaven and the deepest depths of hell, an experience which had changed for ever my outlook on life, in the short space of twenty-eight days. I became an inmate of the first temporary hospital at the Salisbury Road Schools, Plymouth.

One of the most indefatigable workers in the cause of our comfort was Lady Astor, who was affectionately known among us as 'Nancy', and to whom I now record my thanks.

Having been made comfortable in hospital I became concerned for the welfare of my young brother. I was exceedingly worried about him, and fervently prayed that he had escaped the awful fate that had overtaken so many of my stalwart comrades.

My mind was eased on this score by the receipt of a letter from my parents. From this I learnt that he had also arrived safely in England, having been wounded a few days after I had received my *congé* and that he was in a fair way towards recovery.

I conclude this story, holding fond thoughts of that gallant body of adventurers it was my high honour to command as Lance-Corporal, acting Brigadier-General, entirely unofficially, and decidedly unpaid—'The Phantom Brigade'—and finally, by rising to salute the memory of five gallant and unknown gentlemen of the Royal Field Artillery.

Lightning Source UK Ltd.
Milton Keynes UK
UKHW022149090123
415068UK00015B/1980